# Sportuality

## Finding Joy in the Games

### JEANNE HESS

**BALBOA.**
PRESS
A DIVISION OF HAY HOUSE

Article reprinted from DailyOM- Inspirational thoughts for a happy, healthy and fulfilling day. Register for free at www.dailyom.com.

Balboa Press books may be ordered through booksellers or by contacting:

Balboa Press
A Division of Hay House
1663 Liberty Drive
Bloomington, IN 47403
www.balboapress.com
1-(877) 407-4847

Because of the dynamic nature of the Internet, any web addresses or links contained in this book may have changed since publication and may no longer be valid. The views expressed in this work are solely those of the author and do not necessarily reflect the views of the publisher, and the publisher hereby disclaims any responsibility for them.

The author of this book does not dispense medical advice or prescribe the use of any technique as a form of treatment for physical, emotional, or medical problems without the advice of a physician, either directly or indirectly. The intent of the author is only to offer information of a general nature to help you in your quest for emotional and spiritual well-being. In the event you use any of the information in this book for yourself, which is your constitutional right, the author and the publisher assume no responsibility for your actions.

Any people depicted in stock imagery provided by Thinkstock are models, and such images are being used for illustrative purposes only.
Certain stock imagery © Thinkstock.

ISBN: 978-1-4525-4381-9 (sc)
ISBN: 978-1-4525-4382-6 (hc)
ISBN: 978-1-4525-4380-2 (e)

Library of Congress Control Number: 2011962329

Printed in the United States of America

Balboa Press rev. date: 03/27/2012

Dedicated to the joys of my life: Jim, Andrew, and Kevan

# Acknowledgments

Gratitude is at the heart of everything in the following pages. To family, friends, players, and acquaintances who have encouraged me, thank you.

I am most grateful to my husband, Jim, for his understanding and encouragement during this three-year process of bringing *Sportuality* to life. He is my rock and my inspiration and the best sportual partner I could have ever found. Thanks to my sons, Andrew and Kevan, for proving that, indeed, one can live with her heart walking around outside her body. I love you both and revel in your sportual lives!

To my loving parents, thank you for supporting me in all my sporting pursuits in an era when they were not necessarily the norm for girls and young women, for giving me a childhood of love, family, and faith. For the values you instilled, for all the lessons, and for your perseverance through life's trials, you have been a great inspiration. And to my dear Aunt Gerry, who passed through before *Sportuality's* publication. Your prayers and encouragement kept me going. You are now making a difference from the other side!

This book would not exist without the excellence, the understanding, and the articulation of my good friend, peacemaker, and editor, Robert Weir: http://www.robertmweir.com/. From our original meeting at the Department of Peace for Michigan's 6th Congressional District to joining forces in this project, we have grown, laughed, learned, and marveled at the miracles of *Sportuality*. Thank you, Robert, for sharing your genius with me. You are within and throughout these pages, which also share an intention of peace.

To all the wonderful and helpful people at Balboa Press for taking my manuscript and giving it life, I am so thankful that you are on my team.

To all of my teams, coaches, players, and families from the past thirty-two years, thank you for trusting the process and for bringing such joy into my life.

Kalamazoo College, you embody your motto, *Lux Esto* (Be Light). For supporting me as a coach and as a teacher, I am grateful for the career of my dreams. To all of my colleagues who have inspired or encouraged me, even though you may not know it, I feel tremendous gratitude. You are all the joy that is Kalamazoo College.

Great thanks to the Great Lakes Colleges Association (GLCA) for your grant support for my focus group review of the original manuscript. I hope you know how encouraging it was to have your vote of confidence during this process.

To Jack Eppinga, a.k.a. Bearclaw Jack, the artist and creator of Sportuality's cover sculpture art, thank you for engaging with my vision of joy! http://www.bearclawjack.com/. You truly have a gift.

And thank you, Jimmy Buffett, for providing a soundtrack to this crazy life. As you say in An Attitude of Gratitude: "Say thank you with infactatude; it's a brand new day."

This *is* a brand new day, and *thank you* to all who participated in any way with the creation of Sportuality.

# Introduction

**Sportuality (spor-choo-al-i-tee)**

*noun:*

a way of finding joy in the games

**Sportual (spor-choo-uhl)**

*adjective:*

of or pertaining to a person's ability to find joy in the games as a player, a coach, a manager, an official, or a fan

*I had rather hoped the term "sportuality" was unique, but I suppose it's quite obvious if you think about it.*

—Mat Dickey

The arena, the stadium, the court, or the field can be our connection to the One, to the Creator, to the meaning and purpose we seek from deep within. This insight came to me as a child in the 1960s on the cusp of Title IX (enacted in 1972) when I was a self-proclaimed tomboy. The concept was reinforced further when I played as a varsity volleyball athlete at the University of Michigan in the 1970s and again as a collegiate volleyball coach from 1984 to the present 2011, as a college chaplain, and as a mother of two professional baseball athletes.

I am fueled by competition and love of sport. Through sport, I know joy and peace. In sport, I challenge the way our culture uses sport to promote and sustain a war-based paradigm. Thanks to sport,

I have honed my story and heard the stories of others, some of which are included in this book, *Sportuality: Finding Joy in the Games.*

*Sportuality* explores the true meaning and etymology of words such as *competition, spirit, inspiration, conspiracy, humor, enthusiasm,* and others. By reaching back to the roots of these words, *Sportuality* examines how they have been corrupted by modern usage, a revelation that enables the stories to take on a meaning different from current cultural values.

At the same time, the words *sportuality* and *sportual* are new, born in the age of personal media connectivity. Your word processing spellchecker won't recognize them. You won't find them in the dictionary, which is why I created the definitions that appear at the top of this page. You won't find them on Wikipedia—at least not yet. But these words have found their way into the World Wide Web (search and you will find) and, thus, into the web of human consciousness. As computer-game designer and author Mat Dickie says, the words are "unique, but . . . quite obvious if you think about it."

So let's think about it. The words *sportuality* and *sportual* are a blend of *sport* and *spirituality* or *spiritual.* As such, they—and this book—cross disciplines to help readers evolve a higher consciousness, a spiritual aspect, within sport and competition.

## Redefining the Words

### Sport (spohrt)

*noun:*

an athletic activity requiring skill or physical prowess and often a competitive nature; a diversion, recreation, pleasant pastime; jest, fun, mirth, pleasantry, amusement; something treated lightly or tossed about like a plaything; something or someone subject to the whims of fate or circumstances; a sportsman or sportswoman; a person who behaves in a sporting, fair, or admirable manner[1]

**Spiritual (spir-i-choo-uhl)**

*adjective:*

of, pertaining to, or consisting of spirit, incorporeal, not of the body; of or pertaining to the spirit or soul, as distinguished from the physical nature; supernatural; of or pertaining to sacred things or matters; religious; devotional; of or relating to the mind or intellect[2]

**Spirituality (spir-i-choo-al-i-tee)**

*noun:*

the quality or fact of being spiritual[3]

Looking at the definitions for sport, we see elements found in the essence of spiritual and spirituality. Teams have spirit. God intends for us to have fun and be playful; that's why humans created sport, initially for primal hunting and today as games played by teams in organized leagues.

One definition tells us that sport is "something or someone subject to the whims of fate or circumstances," from which sport observers have noted that "on any given day, any team can beat any other team." Another definition says that a sport—a good sport, if you will—is "a person who behaves in a sporting, fair, or admirable manner." Is that not the essence of a spiritual being—"to do unto others . . ." or "to turn the other cheek"? Is that not a way to change the world?

The definitions for spirituality include being "not of the body, supernatural." We ask our sport heroes, whether they be professionals or children (or ourselves) playing in recreational or scholastic leagues, to rise above the game, above the pain, above the heartbreak of defeat and into a higher realm. Fans are devoted to their teams. Teams pray. Sport has ceremony and ritual: an umpire's evocation of "Play ball!" the coin toss at the start of a game, tailgate parties, trophy presentations, and even a wreath of roses placed around the neck of a winning thoroughbred racehorse.

Most of all, practitioners of both sport and spirituality ask that we periodically assess ourselves. Coaches call it a gut-check. Religious communities call it prayer or talking with God. In *Sportuality,* I use a *box score* at the end of each chapter; these are your invitations for reflection about your athletic endeavors and your spiritual nature. I believe that, as you do this, you will find that you are a sportual person.

# Game Plan

# Get Your Program Here

If you've been to a professional game, you've likely heard vendors—the people in the striped coats and the funny hats—hawk: "Program! Get your program here! You can't tell the players without a program! Program! Get your program here!"

In this book, the players are words. Obviously, you might say. But I'm referring to certain key words. These are the words that name each chapter: *communication, spirit, competition, community, enthusiasm, humor, education, religion, holy, sanctuary, sacrifice,* and *victory,* as well as two other key words: *ode* and *joy.*

Now, you may think you know the meaning of these words as readily as you know the number on the jersey or uniform of your favorite player. But as you read this book—this program, if you will—you will see that these words have meanings that may be as unknown to you as this season's roster of rookies. At the beginning of each chapter, I will introduce these key words. You might be surprised by what you learn about each—and how much each contributes to the game that is *sportuality.*

So: "Program! Get your program here! You can't tell the players without a program! Program! Get you program here!"

# Pre-Game

Easter 2009: My oldest son blogs from the minor leagues about the meaning, purpose, and sanctity of baseball, not knowing that I am writing a book about the same thing for all sports. His blog confirms for me that there is something to this idea of sportuality. More importantly, I realize that to view sport from a spiritual perspective can help one understand and work with the stress associated with high levels of performance. My purpose, my want, is for sport to be an active participant in the course of human evolution, not the cause of its destruction or its victim.

This world of play has become somewhat mechanistic and overly analytical, so much so that we no longer *play*. We keep statistics. We analyze them. We manipulate them, and we regurgitate them ad infinitum. Statistics define who we were and who we are and tell us who we need to become. Sportuality is more than statistics. Sportuality helps us define *ourselves*. Sportuality can help us play and find joy in sport again.

## ANDREW'S BLOG

Happy Easter

by Andrew @ 10:26 am. Filed under Andrew Hess

Wishing a Happy Easter to everyone from down here in Lakeland, I am relaxing and enjoying a nice Sunday off. I guess it is fitting that our first off day falls on Easter

Sunday, so that we all get time to sit back and reflect on how fortunate we [players] are to be given the gift to play professional baseball.

For me, it would be nice to be able to spend this day with family, but I have become accustomed to spending Easter away from home and somewhere close to a ballpark. It reminds me of the movie *Bull Durham* when the opening scene has a church organ playing along with a picturesque tour of an empty stadium, and Susan Sarandon saying that this is her religion: *the church of baseball*. To a degree, I find this true for me as well. Not saying that baseball takes the place of religion, but for us it really takes on a different meaning. When you think about it, you have a sanctuary that people come to everyday looking for hope; there is a story that unfolds in each game; and there is plenty that can be translated from the game into everyday life. Baseball has a way of bringing people together and giving hope to the otherwise hopeless.

For example, take my lifelong journey with my favorite team and now current employer, the Detroit Tigers. I assume most people who read this are Tiger fans to some degree, but how many years there in the mid-late nineties did we say, "Alright, this is THE year. We're gonna make the playoffs this year. I can feel it." Then somehow find out that two months into the season, we were mathematically eliminated already. Ha, but did that deter us from our fanhood and abandon the team the next year? No. And why? *Faith*—faith that this season we would win ninety games. Or that Bobby Higginson would finally earn that paycheck, or that maybe we would pick up a big free agent who would win a Cy Young. It took a long time for the relationship to return the favor, but I will never forget what I felt like when I saw that ball leave Maggs' [Magglio Ordóñez] bat and the Tigers were going to the World Series in 2006.

I usually don't like to blend baseball and religion. I think that each is sacred in its own right and usually one is used to amend the deeds done by the other. But when you think about the similarities and how each can be used in life, baseball and religion are not so different. That home run, by the way, probably restored some Detroit fans' faith again, because I'm sure the words "Thank you, God" were uttered throughout.

As Andrew suggests, sportuality resides in and throughout our lives. Indeed, Andrew would not exist on this Earth had it not been for a fateful day in September of 1980 when I tore my right ACL (anterior cruciate ligament, the structure in one's knee that keeps it stable). I was a recent baccalaureate graduate of the University of Michigan and well on my way to entering graduate studies in athletic training at that university. And I was passionate about volleyball. So while being the student trainer at the women's volleyball practice one evening, the men playing on the next court convinced me that I could play with them and keep an eye on the women. As it turned out, on one particularly fateful play, I was able to jump and block my opponent's hit, but my right knee left me at some point during the jump, and I was the one in need of a trainer. Life, as I had planned it, was over.

In 1980, the treatment of choice for a female athlete's post-collegiate career injury was to put a cast on it for six weeks. My only choice at the time was to move home and reconsider my options. After the cast came off, I followed my love of volleyball back into coaching at Ann Arbor Gabriel Richard High School as the junior varsity coach. While as a player, I swore that I would never teach or coach due to what I perceived as my lack of patience. But when my friend and teammate Carol Ratza got the varsity job at Gabriel Richard, her first call was to me: "Hey, Jeanne, you're not doing anything else. Do you wanna be my JV coach?" Now, years later, I am comfortable advising the student-athletes and my advisees at Kalamazoo College, where I am the women's volleyball coach, that the best jobs find *you*. But back then, on the phone with Carol, the thought that something miraculous had happened did not occur to me. I said yes anyway.

Thus, I was led down this crazy, addictive path of coaching, eventually reaping, in a thirty-year career, all the fruits of the spirit—patience being paramount among them.

It was there at Ann Arbor Gabriel Richard High School where I met Jim Hess, the highly successful girls' basketball and softball coach, who later became my husband. Jim and I married in 1982 and almost immediately moved to Kalamazoo so that he could take a position at Western Michigan University as head women's basketball coach. Kalamazoo College volleyball came calling to me not long afterward, and Andrew, the future Detroit Tiger then in the womb, went through my entire first season with me, being born six days after our final game in 1984.

From then, fast forwarding to now, it would seem that our lives are all about sport—yet they are not. Our lives are more than sport. They are sportual. Through our relationships, our jobs, and our studies, we have sought peace, social justice, equality, and joy, while also seeking the success and physical excellence demanded by sport.

The following pages present what I have learned in twenty-eight years of coaching collegiate volleyball and raising two sons through all kinds of sports and into the professional ranks of baseball. Ralph Waldo Emerson said, "It is a happy talent to know how to play." Indeed. My joy, my purpose, and my happiness lie in the play available to me in this miraculous life.

It is my hope that by sharing this work you will access your own sportual story and, therefore, the joy that is your birthright. I know you have one! Simply from talking with others about sportuality, I find that everyone has stories from sport that feed their spirit—*and* they want to share them!

## Sportual Stories

Story offers every person the chance to make a better world through the power of words. "True stories of ordinary people are the most inspiring experiences we share. Stories talk about action and stories inspire action," writes Christina Baldwin in *Storycatcher: Making Sense of our Lives through the Power and Practice of Story*. [4]

Sportual stories appear throughout this book. Some are personal, and others are borrowed, but each is intended to spark your sportuality and to have you recall moments when you also may have felt sportual. Here's the first; it's one of mine.

## Sportuality's Helping Hands

The journey to baseball's Major League for the majority of players in the system is actually a pilgrimage that requires sacrifice and patience. While the players drafted in the first round make the headlines, there are forty-nine draft rounds after that. Just like the tip of the iceberg, the ones who make the news—and the money—are only a small percentage of the entire organization.

Our Andrew, who writes with his left hand and throws with his right, was selected in the nineteenth round by the Detroit Tigers as a pitcher despite having a sore, impinged shoulder. With his undergraduate education behind him at the University of Michigan, Andrew went to Lakeland, Florida, to begin the MLB journey. He spent the first summer rehabbing and didn't see much action, but after healing, he has found himself and his desire to achieve at the highest levels. This could be a story of simple achievement, but it goes far beyond the physical and mental to the sportual.

Andrew was born in November 1984, just days after my beloved Detroit Tigers won the World Series for the first time in nearly two decades. I spent those last few weeks of my pregnancy intent upon the Tigers' success, mostly because I couldn't move from the recliner after a few hours of coaching each day.

Andrew came into a family with a long history of fondness for the Tigers. My parents grew up as Tiger fans in Detroit, and Jim has special memories of his dad taking him to his first Tiger game as a child. My favorite childhood recollections are of baseball, of the Tigers in the 1960s, and of exhausting the batteries in my transistor radio while listening to the night games as I fell to sleep.

We have photos of Andrew as a baby in Tiger gear, and the most joyful one was taken when *his* dad took him to *his* first game at Tiger Stadium at age two. One particularly funny photograph is of Andrew, at six months, which had been hidden in his memorabilia box, wearing his Tiger "uniform" and hat, clutching a mini-bat. The picture had been signed by three Tigers from that era: Darrell Evans, Manny Castillo, and Mike Laga, all members of the 1984 World Series Championship team.

Was Andrew destined to follow the baseball path because of his parents' influence? Or did he choose to because of his God-given athletic talent? Who knows? As Forrest Gump would say years later, "I think maybe it's both." What I do know is that Andrew knows joy and can well articulate the meaning and purpose within the game. He's engaged in the journey on multiple levels, including the sportual level and that's what matters now. On the field, he displays his gifts as a thrower, and in his blog, he employs his writing to share his experiences and joy in the game with others.

But this baseball story doesn't end there. Two years after Andrew's draft experience, we went through the same thing with our second son, Kevan. And if I told you that he was drafted by the Tigers as a pitcher, you might think I, like Forrest Gump, was making this up for the sake of a good story. Well, it's true. He has stats, photos, and a story of his own—even a rookie card now. But for me, as I look at a series of meaningful photos of Andrew and Kevan displayed on shelves in our home, the very idea of these brothers playing professional baseball together appeared during their childhood.

The first photo, on the top shelf, is of Andrew at about eighteen months in a solitary, pensive pose, perched upon a rock on the shore of Lake Michigan in the northwestern part of the state. The second photo, on the middle shelf, is Andrew at age five and Kevan at two walking hand in hand on the beach at South Haven toward Lake Michigan. Andrew is slightly ahead of Kevan and appears to be pulling him toward the water. The last photo, on the bottom shelf and the one that lit the "aha" light for me, is of them building a sand castle together on a beach in the Bahamas. Andrew was ten, and Kevan was seven.

Now, fifteen years later, they are playing together again, and I see the pattern of those photos replicated in the young men they are now. There is Andrew, alone at first, paving the way into the Tiger farm system. Then, he is leading Kevan through the process. And finally, they are playing together in the Tigers' system, hopefully helping to build the Tigers into another World Series contender.

Theirs is a perfect sportual story.

# Warm-Up: Ode to Joy

**Ode ('od)**

*noun:*

a lyric poem that expresses a noble feeling with dignity; originally a poem intended to be sung[5]

**Joy ('joi)**

*noun:*

intense, ecstatic, or exultant happiness or pleasure[6]

*Joy runs deeper than mere pleasure; especially in a spiritual context, it runs deep into the core of us, and radiates throughout. It is the response of something deep in the soul to someone (such as God or a loved one) or something (such as liberation) supremely, even overpoweringly, wonderful.*

—Robert Longman, Jr.

*Ancient Egyptians believed that upon death they would be asked two questions and their answers would determine whether they could continue their journey in the afterlife. The first question was, 'Did you bring joy?' The second was, 'Did you find joy?'*

—Dr. Leo Buscaglia

*There is no beautifier of complexion, or form, or behavior, like the wish
to scatter joy and not pain around us.*

—Ralph Waldo Emerson

*Joy is a net of love by which you can catch souls. A joyful heart is the
inevitable result of a heart burning with love.*

—Mother Teresa

## Can You Feel This?

I am in Omaha, Nebraska, in December 2008 at the semi-finals of the
NCAA Division I volleyball championships.

The unbelievable is happening. Penn State, currently undefeated
and who has not lost even a set in any match during the entire season,
is tied with Nebraska, two sets to two in a best-of-five match. A record
crowd for volleyball of 17,000 fans, mainly from Nebraska, are beyond
themselves with elation. They are a factor in their team's success, and
they know it. The place, as they say, is rockin'. Emotions are high, and
each contact of the ball is filled with purpose for both teams as the
score stays close for the entire fifth set. It is one of those moments
when time stands still, where the "zone" is real. Omaha's Qwest Center
is literally shaking.

As an attendee at the American Volleyball Coaches Association
convention during this event, I am seated among other coaches, who
are always the last to share emotions during someone else's game.
Why? Because coaches simply don't do that. They observe, analyze,
and control. This contest, however, takes us beyond the typical contest,
and everyone in my section joins in the pandemonium.

And here comes the cool part. Seated next to me is Lynn Ray Boren,
the head coach from Gallaudet University in Washington, DC, a school
for the hearing impaired. Being deaf himself, Lynn cannot hear the
roar that defines this sportual moment for me. But with the score tied

at 11-11 in set five, the deciding set in this best three-out-of-five event, everyone in the arena is on their feet, including the coaches.

Time-out.

The crowd is shouting, standing, clapping, roaring. The band is playing. Cheerleaders are dancing. I feel goose bumps (recalling the scene, I still can bring back the goose bumps). I turn to Lynn Ray, smile, open my arms and gesture toward the arena. Knowing he can read lips, I say, "Can you *feel* this?" He smiles a huge smile, puts one hand over his heart, and also gestures around the arena. He says "I can *feel* this!"

In *Outliers: The Story of Success,* Malcolm Gladwell talks about needing exact timing for certain events to happen.[7] That moment in Nebraska was one of those when all senses blended together and the game elevated all of us to an unbelievable oneness.

Sportuality doesn't discriminate between sizes, races, genders, classes, ages, abilities, or particular sport. Sportuality is available to all—to the One—to anyone who asks.

Watching that game and silently communicating with Lynn Ray, it suddenly occurred to me that my life was perfect, and happiness comes from knowing that *each* moment is perfect!

Often a gap in time exists between an event and that type of significant realization. For example, I had spent fifteen years wishing I had my ACL back. In actuality, I was slowly waking up to my sportuality and finally becoming thankful—even joyful—that I tore my ACL.

We often confuse joy with happiness. But while happiness is temporary, joy is a state of being. Jesus said, "Ask and it shall be given you; seek and you shall find; knock and it shall be opened unto you."[8] When we consciously seek joy, we cannot help but manifest it in our lives. For some, joy might come through an injury or a setback. For some, it comes in the midst of struggle, pain, and sweat. And, for some, it comes in the simple act of playing the game. Regardless of the situation, joy is always available.

In *The Little Book of Big Questions,* Dianna Booher writes, "Happiness happens from the outside; it depends on other people, events, results. Joy bubbles up from the inside; it originates with attitude. Happiness is in the circumstances; joy is in the heart. Happiness may not happen; joy is a promise from God."[9]

Similarly, French author Leon Bloy writes, "Joy is the most infallible sign of the presence of God."[10] We can come to an awareness of God through the joy we feel when playing the game. We don't name the joy, but we love a sport or resonate with a sport because we feel the joy of the sport. And when we do, we feel, as Bloy states, the presence of God.

I don't know that we understand this connection, but I believe that in order to know God, we need to know joy. And if we find joy in the sport we play, we are connecting with God through sport. That is sportuality. Games = joy = our connection with God. Through sport—and sportuality—we sense our Oneness with God as well as our Oneness with all other people, including those we label as "opponents."

## Universal Joy

In her book *Who Is God? The Soul's Road Home*, teacher and author Irma Zaleski explores joy in this way: "Because joy is an inner experience of the presence of God—a relationship—it is impossible to categorize it or define it in words. Like love itself, it cannot be taught. Each human being must find his or her own path to its door. For a few it may be a 'high road' of contemplation, of ecstasy and bliss. To most of us, however, joy comes in small doses, in short, faint glimpses of the Mystery of God present in the midst of our ordinary lives."[11]

Admittedly, Dr. Zaleski did not have sport at her core as she penned those words, but as we will see, sport can inspire ecstasy and bliss in our ordinary lives. Sport can help us realize, as Indian poet Rabindranath Tagore pointed out, "joy is everywhere."

> *And joy is everywhere;*
> *It is in the Earth's green covering of grass;*
> *In the blue serenity of the Sky;*
> *In the reckless exuberance of Spring;*
> *In the severe abstinence of grey Winter;*
> *In the Living flesh that animates our bodily frame;*

*In the perfect poise of the Human figure, noble and*
*upright;*
*In Living;*
*In the exercise of all our powers;*
*In the acquisition of Knowledge;*
*In fighting evils . . . .*
*Joy is there*
*Everywhere.*
—Rabindranath Tagore, Indian Poet[12]

## The Path to Joy

WASHINGTON, DC—January 20, 2009. Inauguration Day in the United States.

President Barack Obama has won an historic election, worked to assemble his "team," and has gone about the business of reuniting and healing this wounded nation. Is it simply coincidence that he plays basketball, a team sport?

The January 13, 2009, issue of *Sports Illustrated* ran an article by Alexander Wolff about the upcoming inauguration. He wrote: "Maybe Barack Obama needed to be a community organizer to become a U.S. Senator. And maybe, just maybe, Americans chose him as their next president because they too have come to recognize that in the end it's not about you, it's about the team. Perhaps on Tuesday he will say it: Come, let us get swept up in the moment. Let us create and sustain the trance."[13]

I find it interesting that YouTube has had several thousand hits on Obama's high school championship game when, as a substitute, he got in only at the end of the game when his team had a winning lead, made a layup, and missed a free throw. Is it coincidence—or because of joy—that he connected with people along the campaign trail with friendly shoot-arounds or pick-up games? Is it also coincidence that whenever you see media reports of these games he is always smiling? To me, there is no doubt that our president, the leader of the free world, finds joy in sport just like millions of other men and women around the globe, regardless of their publicity status or political profile.

In thirty years of coaching other people's children while raising my own, I have found that one of the deepest held desires for parents is to see their children happy. While I agree, I will go a step further and submit that all parents, whether they acknowledge it or not, really wish *joy* for their children, even if it doesn't come wrapped up and tied with the bow of comfort and happiness. It is that joy expressed by Kalamazoo poet Mark Nepo in "About Joy" in which wonder and joy are all that we have left at the end of all our striving and life experience:

> *Often, what keeps us from joy is the menacing assumption*
> *that life is happening other than where we are. So we are*
> *always leaving, running from or running to. All the while,*
> *joy rises like summer wind, waiting for us to grow in the*
> *open, large as willows it can sing through. Yet failing to*
> *grow in the open, we can be worn to it. Working with*
> *what we're given till it wears us through seems to be the*
> *grace we resist. Still, like everyone, I have spent so much*
> *of my life fearing pain that I have seldom felt things all*
> *the way through. And falling through more than working*
> *through, I've learned that if we can stay true to our*
> *experience and to each other, and face the spirit that*
> *experience and love carry, we will eventually be reduced*
> *to joy. Like cliffs worn to their beauty by the pounding of*
> *the sea, if we can hold each other up, all that will be left*
> *will be wonder and joy.* [14]

"If we can hold each other up." Exactly. What is a team but others who hold us up, or lift us up, emotionally, physically, mentally and spiritually? In sport, this can include coaches and other players, fans and family, and, to some extent, even media. Consider teams of which you've been a member and recall the intensity of those relationships as you held each other up.

## Engaging the Game

I have found that children most often reflect their parent's ideas of joy, so it is no wonder that "the nut doesn't fall far from the family tree." And it is no wonder that sport is where my children have found their joy—at least for now. While it was not a conscious choice in my younger years to value the meaning and purpose of sport, it has proved for me to be the greatest joy of my life and, indeed, my life path.

As a female child born in the 1950s, I did not see sport as a mainstream career option. But as a teen on the cusp of Title IX, doors opened and provided opportunities for me and other women that had been previously reserved for men. In the nearly forty years since President Richard Nixon signed Title IX into law, women have made great strides in the United States, including in the arena of sport. But the one stride so near to my heart is that women have moved from being mere spectators—or at best, cheerleaders—and can now participate more completely and, thus, feel and experience those moments of exhilaration. Women can now feel sportuality, the result of finding joy in *playing* the games.

However, no matter how much I believe in and support Title IX, I write not for purposes of gender balance or equality, per se. Rather, I write for an even greater awareness: that *all* might know and experience the great joy of really, truly, and deeply engaging in the game.

## Peacefully Dwelling within Sport

As kids, we're introduced to different games or sports, and we're either repulsed by them or they settle deeply into our bones. We may continue with a favorite sport throughout our lifetimes as paid players, coaches, announcers, and executives. Or we may learn the sport's elementary lessons and move on, as President Obama has with basketball, to use sport as a metaphor and teaching tool for teamwork, cooperation, sharing, and even joy.

When we persevere in a particular sport, even at an amateur level, we might ask ourselves: "Why? What keeps us coming back?" Most likely, it is a combination of things: a coach's influence, our own physical aptitude, positive role models, conditions and circumstances, support from our family, perhaps how we *feel* when we play. All are significant factors, to be sure, but the one thing that I usually return to is this phenomenon I call "sportuality"—the ability to find joy in playing the game.

In the Introduction to his bestseller *Sacred Hoops*, basketball coach Phil Jackson quotes the Buddha: "Unceasing change turns the wheel of life, and so reality is shown in all its many forms. Peaceful dwelling as change itself liberates all suffering sentient beings and brings them great joy."[15] Some people have judged Jackson's quiet demeanor. Some of his players have questioned why he would encourage team meditation and quote the Buddha, a physical image of God. But Jackson has found a mystical joy in what he does. He understands that the change about which the Buddha speaks is an inevitable part of sport: players change teams, teams change players and coaches, teams change their offensive and defensive programs, injuries force changes. This is the "unceasing change" of which the Buddha speaks.

But Jackson has learned that stress, a common reaction to change, is a choice. This awareness and Jackson's willingness to *allow* the game to happen, rather than *force* the game to happen according to unilateral expectations, has allowed Jackson and his teams to compete on a world stage and win at the highest level. Because of his unique perspective, Jackson is not a prototypical basketball coach. He's huge and could use his physical presence to an apparent advantage, but, rather, he seeks advantage in a sportual way. He doesn't rip his coat off and throw it onto a chair. He's introspective, meditative. And he understands the concept of finding joy in the game and of finding, through joy, his connection with God.

To the Buddha's quote, Jackson adds his own thought: "It's the 'peaceful dwelling' that often gets to me as I squirm under the changes rather than embracing them. This work-in-progress is a terrific challenge for me as I get a chance to allow players to develop at their own rates, to accept defeat with victory, and to allow a peaceful dwelling to bring great joy."[16]

## Getting into the Game

I invite you to come with me on this journey of exploration of sport. You may find that you will begin to consider sport differently, converting your perception of it from a mere pastime into a sportual endeavor with meaning and purpose.

We'll question together: Why are you drawn to volleyball, basketball, golf, bowling, or baseball . . . wrestling, running, or football . . . equestrian, cycling, or swimming . . . skiing, skating, or sledding . . . exercise and physical exertion? Whether or not we find answers, don't be surprised if you enter into unbridled joy!

Consider, for example, moments when you were moved by sport. Where were you when:

- The Boston Red Sox beat the New York Yankees in Fenway Park in the seventh game of the American League playoffs in 2004 and broke the infamous Curse of the Bambino?

- The historic "Ice Bowl" happened in Green Bay?

- Hank Aaron broke the Babe's home run record?

- The USA won the World Cup in Women's Soccer?

- The USA men's hockey team defeated the favored Russian team in The Miracle on Ice?

- Armando Galarraga pitched a "near perfect" game for the Detroit Tigers?

- *Your* team won the Super Bowl, the World Series, the NBA Championship, or the NCAA Championship, or a scholastic or city league title?

Have you personally tasted the miracle of a Hail Mary pass, a buzzer-beater half-court shot, or a totally unexpected upset?

What's your sportual story? You know the one I mean. The one you play over and over in your memory—in slow motion. It bubbles up from inside of you. It has affected your journey, and you've told it so many times it has become part of your ongoing life story, and your buddies practically know it by heart, too. This is the story that connects you to everyone and everything—so much so that when you think, "Was that Heaven?" the sportual answer comes back as "Yes . . . it was!"

As is the case with Dawn Todd's story, based on her experience while playing varsity softball at Kalamazoo College. In addition to being the head women's volleyball coach, I also served as the assistant softball coach for a period of five years. My role was largely to inspire and motivate while hitting fly balls to the outfielders. One of the stories I would tell the team was that of the optimist and pessimist, often called the "Pony Story." Its message is that when we inspire with intention, we never know how far our words will reach.

To help you understand—and to give an example of a sportual story—the following is the story that Dawn shared with me well after her graduation. While I was present as she fell with the injury she writes about, and was there at her commencement ceremony when she walked across the stage to receive her diploma (a goal that kept her moving forward in physical therapy), I did not realize that the incident and its subsequent activities had such a profound effect on her life view.

## Dawn's Sportual Story

Thus, Dawn's story was a gift to me too. As I have remained in coaching, I realized that what I might consider lightly might just be that "aha" moment for an athlete. Dawn's message of finding joy in adversity or what the Chinese proverb describes as "opportunity being present in challenge" is a universal truth that can change us forever for the better—if we allow ourselves to enter into sportuality.

Finding My Pony
Dawn Todd
January 21, 2002

*A mother and father were troubled with the behaviors of their two young sons. Although they were identical twins, they were essentially exact opposites. One was an optimist, and the other a clear-cut pessimist. One day, in an effort to test their different behaviors, the parents filled the pessimist's room with all of the latest toys they could find, which they thought would make him happy. The parents then filled the optimist's room with horse manure, scattering it about the floor. When the boys arrived home from school, the pessimist went to his room, opened the door and eagerly began to play with his toys. It didn't take long before the boy was complaining that the batteries had died, the toys were too slow, and some were easily breakable. The mother and father were disappointed that he hadn't responded more appreciatively. The optimist then ran to his room, opened the door, and found the floor covered in manure. "Oh boy, oh boy!!!" the son cried. The parents were baffled by his reaction, and asked him why he showed so much excitement over the pile of manure. The optimist's reply was, "If there's manure in here, that means there's gotta be a pony somewhere!"*

The story of the optimist and the pessimist was first shared with me when I was a sophomore in college by Coach Hess, for whom I hold a great deal of admiration and respect. The relevance and meaning of this story, however, was not fully realized until two years later when I was dealing with a very difficult time in my life.

In my senior year of college, I was a four-year starter and two-year captain on the varsity softball team, enjoying and fulfilling the responsibilities of my role as a leader to my teammates and looking to end my career with one of my best seasons ever. I had envisioned the end of my collegiate playing days many times, but never imagined that it would happen so suddenly and so painfully, both physically and emotionally.

It was the second inning of the nightcap against a league rival—a game that I had been looking forward to since the first days of conditioning in the fall. I was on first base after being walked by the pitcher, anticipating the actions of my teammate, who was now at the plate. I took my leadoff on the first pitch—a ball. I returned to the bag, ready to make my jump on the next pitch. I exploded off the base toward second when my teammate hit a low line-drive to right field. Halfway between the bases I opened my body to the play to see if the ball had been caught, or if it had hit the ground—to see if I could advance to second, or if I had to hustle back to first. Thinking the ball would be caught, I made a move toward first base, but when the ball skipped on the ground in front of the right fielder, I attempted to quickly shift my momentum back in the opposite direction.

Not all of my body responded to my command. As I pivoted my body and shifted my weight forward, my left foot stayed planted in the ground, and I heard the two loudest pops I had ever heard in my life, and then felt an explosion in my left knee. My body crumpled to the dirt, and the day's light darkened behind my eyes; my mind was flooded with memories of games that had passed, and blanked with visions of those yet to come. I tried everything in my power to get up. To take it back. To make it go away. But in my broken heart, I knew it was all over for me.

Five games left to go in my entire career, and I would never set foot on the field as a collegiate athlete again. My initial reactions to this devastating injury were, "How could this happen to me? Why was I cheated of the last games of my career? Why couldn't it happen to someone who has less heart and passion for the game?"

I quickly realized, however, that I still had an important role to play for my team, and that I could not become consumed with self-pity and despair. As the captain, I had a duty to fulfill as the leader and motivating spirit of my teammates; I was determined to do so until the season had officially ended for everyone, not just me. We still had five games to play, and if I was unable to lead my team by my actions from the playing field, I nonetheless needed to play the part of the mental and emotional leader, supporting and encouraging from the dugout.

One month after my injury occurred, I underwent ACL reconstruction and meniscal repair on my knee. At this point, God was really challenging my strength, character, and integrity as a human being, as I was also experiencing a number of other emotionally charging and draining events in my life: the suicide of a family member, the death of our family pet, and college graduation just two weeks around the corner. To dig deep enough within myself to accept the challenges of rehabilitation and overcome the hardships of my new disability, while at the same time deal with these other life-changing events, was an obstacle unlike any I had ever faced before.

During the rehabilitation phase I really began to take time to reflect upon myself. I reflected mostly upon the things that I had taken for granted all my life—the physical abilities that I now had to struggle with, yet watched other people do with mindless ease: walking, jogging, jumping, riding a bike, and competing.

I also reflected on the most important things I'd taken for granted—the relationships that I had developed with so many important people in my life: family, friends, teachers, professors, coaches, and teammates.

I knew that I would never again fail to be thankful for all of the gifts I had been given.

While I felt that I was making a concerted effort to make the best of the difficult situation I was in at the time, the message and moral of the story of the optimist and the pessimist didn't hit me hard until three weeks post-op when I was undergoing rehabilitation in the pool with my physical therapist.

I had just finished an hour-long therapy session and slowly made my way out of the pool to the locker room—holding onto walls and handrails to make sure I didn't lose my footing on the wet tiles. As I entered the locker room to rinse off in the shower, I heard a mother talking to her young daughter in the bathroom stall. She said, "Come on, you need to get in the shower before you get into the pool."

Overhearing this, I quickly slipped into the one shower that was available and began to rinse off. Because of my impatience at the time, I didn't want to wait for someone else to use the shower before me. As I snuck in behind the curtain, the stall door opened, and I heard the girl say, "Hey! I was going in there!"

I replied to her, "Sorry, I'll be really quick."

She pulled the curtain back and said, "That's okay. I don't really like showers anyway. The water's too cold in there for me." With this, I showed her how to turn on the warm water, and she seemed pleased.

"I really like your swimsuit," she said of my blue and green tye-dyed Speedo.

"Thanks a lot," I said. "I like yours too."

I then got out of the shower, and it was at this moment I realized that this little girl, no more than seven or eight years old, was using a walker with wheels for her mobility. Her mother then appeared from around the corner—also using a walker on wheels.

The girl then asked me with a great deal of enthusiasm, "Did you see me floating the other day? I was floating all by myself. My therapist was holding me up, and then she lowered her arms down in the water, and I was floating on my back all by myself!"

When I answered that I hadn't seen her float, but I congratulated her all the same, I asked her what her name was. This was when nothing short of an act of God occurred.

"My name is Ashley. Do you want to see my pony?"

I told her that I would love to see her pony, so she disappeared into the locker section and reappeared a few moments later holding Derby, a small Beanie Baby pony—the exact same one that I have kept on my desk ever since I was told the story of the optimist and the pessimist. The exact same one that has constantly reminded me that when nothing seems to be going right in my life, there is always a light at the end of the tunnel, and something good will result from the seemingly bad. *The exact same one.*

Ashley then headed off to the pool for her therapy. All I could do was sit in the locker room, put my head in my hands, and sob.

I was crying not for myself, for it was then I realized I had absolutely nothing to feel sorry for myself about. I cried for this little girl who would never know all of the things I had known: swimming with friends, running through the park, and playing sports competitively. I had known twenty-two years without hardships, without challenges, without roadblocks. And I had never given it a second thought until this very moment.

I continued to cry silently into my towel. For all of the things that this little girl has known, that I had never even dreamed possible. She has known eight years of struggle. Determination. Overcoming the odds when almost everything seemed against her. She has known about reveling in the minute joys and details, and learning to live, *and be happy*, with what God has given her.

At a time when I needed it most in my life, an eight-year-old child, whose pony was the small, seemingly simple accomplishments in life, helped me to find my own.

I had been riding it for nearly twenty-three years, and didn't know it until that day.

When Dawn played at Kalamazoo College, she was a happy, joy-filled player. Now, several years after graduation and with a young child of her own, Dawn is struggling within a career that doesn't bring her joy. But unlike the heroic stories common to earlier generations who endured hardships and suffering endlessly, she is seeking a better, more joyful way.

From her ongoing communications with me, I believe that Dawn will find her joy again in sport—either through herself or through her son or by sportually giving to others. Her anterior cruciate ligament (ACL) has been repaired, and she has walked in multi-day breast cancer fundraisers. She has volunteered to coach persons in wheelchairs who play ball on a rubber field that facilitates their wheeled mobility. But she has also given up that role for the sake of her job and time with her son. Her choice was precipitated by financial necessity and love. But I also believe that Dawn is one of those people who need to be in the game. I believe she will find a way to do what she loves while also caring for the family she loves. She will get back on her pony.

# Box Score: Write Your Sportual Story

Throughout this book, I will invite you to take a look at your own box score, to assess your statistics regarding sportuality. Here is your first invitation.

> **BOX SCORE:**
>
> Inspired by Dawn, now take some time and write your sportual story.

# FIRST QUARTER: Communication and Spirit

# Communication
## "to make common"
## (all-encompassing)

Com-mu-ni-cate (ke-'myu-ne-kat)

*verb (used with object):*

to impart knowledge; to make known; to administer the Eucharist; to share in or partake of

*verb (used without an object):*

to give, express, or interchange thoughts, feelings, information by writing or speaking; to be joined or connected; to take part or participate; to partake of the Eucharist.

*origin*

Latin *communicare* to impart, make common[17]

*The words that enlighten the soul are more precious than jewels.*
                                        —Hazrat Inayat Khan

# Redefining the Word

My five years of study in Latin—for what I thought might be a career in medicine—left me with an intense interest in word meaning and etymology. When we peel words back to the original meaning, they provide us with an intent that often differs from current cultural thought and offer a level of understanding that enlightens the soul. Throughout my coaching career, I have been collecting these particular words and their requisite stories. It is through them that I seek and find spiritual meaning, stories, and, yes . . . joy.

For example, in the process of creating this book, I had the notion to include the word *communication* as the key concept in the chapter I had intended to call "the meaning of words." Most of the definitions in this chapter pertain to our common understanding: "to impart or share knowledge, information, thoughts, and feelings." But as I observed the inclusion of the Eucharist among the definitions, the *real* and spiritual meaning emerged and went to my very core. I experienced the "aha" moment I needed to put it all together. To me, as a Eucharistic minister in my faith, receiving the Eucharist, the body and blood of Christ, represents the ultimate communication: "to commune—or be one—with the Creator." I believe that is the ultimate purpose of this life.

While you may or may not believe in the Eucharist as I do, you probably do understand communication as a way of connection with other humans. Communication is not necessarily about *what* message we communicate but rather the spirit or intention in which we convey that message. As is shown in the etymological origin of the word, communication means "to make common" so that all can better share and partake in oneness.

Now consider what players and coaches do as a team: They come together for a common purpose. At first glance, it would appear that they come together to defeat opponents and win games. To do this, they impart information: techniques, strategies, plays. They practice. They laugh and cajole, critique and suggest improvements. When we look at the way teams communicate messages, we see that, in the grand scheme of things, playing sport on a team is a way of communing and becoming one with others.

# Jimmy Buffett: Guru of Messages and Meaning

Since 1978, I have been enamored with the communication and storytelling of pop musician Jimmy Buffett, who I value as a spiritual genius because he finds meaning and purpose in everything from baseball to Hurricane Katrina. Admittedly, I began listening to Jimmy's music after hearing "Why Don't We Get Drunk and Screw" and his signature tune "Margaritaville," but I believe we've evolved together and reached a higher level of communication through some of his later tunes like "Breathe In, Breathe Out, Move On," "A Trip Around the Sun," "Take the Weather with You," and "Wings." In fact, during his forty-year career of musical storytelling, Jimmy has contemplated almost every human action or story in a song. Not a week goes by when I don't say to someone, "Jimmy Buffett has a line for that." And while some choose to use quotes from Winston Churchill or Shakespeare or even Yogi Berra, I quote Jimmy.

I consider Jimmy to be a rather sportual fellow as well. He even takes credit for removing the Curse of the Bambino (supposedly, Boston's decision to sell the great Babe Ruth to the Yankees in the off-season of 1919-1920 has resulted in the Sox not winning a world series for a record eighty-six years, from 1918 to 2004) during his summer 2004 concert at Fenway Park just before he sang "Take Me Out to the Ball Game" as part of his set list in what he called a "Chicken Skin Moment." (Note: There are some who believe Chicken Skin, or goose bumps, to be the presence of the Holy Spirit—and the Red Sox *did* win the World Series that year for the first time in a century.)

Jimmy's words and subsequent stories helped me find words to create my musings that I spoke at a team banquet following an 8-22 season. Both of my sons attended this particular banquet, and I wanted to speak to them and thank them publicly for their influence on me and my coaching life. So I used a fun Jimmy tune titled, "We Are the People Our Parents Warned Us About."

I told my sons I was proud of them and their accomplishments in sport and academics, and also of who they had become. I then extrapolated that idea to the team parents in attendance. "You are now seeing the potential and the strength in your daughters, and that is what this time is all about," I said.

In "Little Miss Magic," Jimmy had a perfect line for that moment too, referencing how his daughter would grow into a confident, free-thinking, successful woman.

I told the parents, "Rest assured that you can take immense pride in these young women and who they are and who they are becoming. I certainly do. So, parents, thank you for everything . . . from the bottom of my heart."

I then used one of Jimmy's sport references in the song "Growing Older but Not Up" to thank our trainer, Monica Lininger, who cared for all of our many health needs during the season. Not only did this fit for Monica, but it also described Dawn's story and the eventual story of the 2009 ESPY Inspiration award winners: the women softball players from Oregon State whose story appears in the Spirit chapter.

Then as I introduced each class, freshmen through seniors, Jimmy's lines and lyrics helped to frame the meaning and purpose of our team time together. He inspired me to infuse a bit of myself and my passion into the celebration of our season. Jimmy's words helped to transform a load of losses into belief, connection, meaning, and purpose. I remain grateful for that sportual moment.

Months later, I would hear from a Buffett-resistant parent that she had even become a fan because of the depth and meaning of his stories and how they fit within team culture.

## Language

Language continued to be the guiding principle of the Kalamazoo College volleyball team as we traveled to China in the summer of 2009. We had a chance to experience the culture, the people, and the country with an ultimate intent of elevating our game. The Shanghai Sports Institute hosted our delegation of nineteen that included ten players, myself, our athletic director, four moms, and three chaperones.

Practice and competition happened on a daily basis during our ten-day stay on their campus. Some of those competitions were with the teams who trained there as part of the Shanghai Volleyball Club, the volleyball division of the Sports Institute, which is the official sport club for the entire province. However, we did not compete with their senior team, who performs at a professional world-class level. Instead, the leadership at the Institute had our college-age women compete with their youth team, comprised of high school girls, ages sixteen to nineteen, who were still a very formidable opponent.

Prior to our first competition, I had told the Institute's coaches that we were without some players due to illness and injury. As we entered the gym, Xiao came up to me and, in broken English, said, "My coach said I play with you." Xiao was a younger member of the senior team, whose role was to perform mainly in practice as a setter.

I could immediately predict that there was going to be a large communication barrier—or maybe I should say a *language* barrier— between our two teams, but this was a great opportunity to both experience the Chinese volleyball culture from the inside and to bust current paradigms of communication in sport. I inserted Xiao into our lineup as an outside hitter (which was not her primary position) for the first game and as a setter for the second game. Our players responded with increased eye contact, one-syllable commands and calls, more hand signals, and lots of smiles.

Later, the team would tell me that it was easy playing with Xiao. They overcame what might have been a communication challenge and turned to their common language of volleyball. They replaced our currently held paradigm of speaking English terms for all our movements with the greater knowledge of simply knowing what to do and trusting that others on the team, through Oneness, would know too. Our game elevated that day because of that realization. They realized joy in the game, and I realized then that maybe joy doesn't come from winning or from all the outcomes, the wins, the press, the media, or the glory that sport represents in our culture. Maybe, I surmised, joy originates within.

# The Universal Language of Sport

One of the greatest lessons the team learned on that trip was that volleyball is a universal language. And one of the greatest lessons I learned is that that the best communication in all of sport doesn't even have words. In volleyball, when you want to communicate with another about your game or simply to ready yourself for the game, we will often play pepper, a back-and-forth sparring with the ball. We communicate through our actions, our control of the ball, a demonstration of our skill, hustle, and joy, and by sharing our common love of the game.

This happens at the end of the movie *Field of Dreams* when Kevin Costner's character, Ray, asks his father (the "ghost") if he wants to "have a catch." Years of pain and estrangement slip away with one simple game of catch under the lights on a summer evening in Iowa as the movie scenes fade into the credits. Even pop-culture "Life Is Good" creators Bert and John Jacobs in their book *Life Is Good: Simple Words from Jake and Rocket* say, "Sometimes the best conversation is a game of catch."[18] Simple, yet so profound and so true.

In his book *The Seven Habits of Highly Effective People*, Stephen Covey weaves the theme of paradigm shifts throughout the manuscript. Since learning the Seven Habits soon after its publication in the early 1990s, I find that these shifts are omnipresent in every sports-themed movie I've ever seen—for that matter, in most non-sports-themed movies as well. Why, even *The Wizard of Oz* represents the grandest spiritual paradigm shift we can experience. Dorothy, the Tin Man, the Lion, and the Scarecrow are all about consciously participating in the journey, waking up and living a more authentic life, and realizing that our true power is already within us.

The movie *Bang the Drum Slowly* may actually be "more about baseball than death" and is, in fact, suggests film critic Roger Ebert, "the ultimate baseball movie." The story takes place during the last season on this Earth of one Bruce Pearson, an earnest but dumb catcher from Georgia who learns, in the movie's first scene, that he is suffering from an incurable disease. The movie is about that season and about his friendship with Henry Wiggen, a pitcher, who undertakes to see that Bruce at least lives his last months with some dignity, some joy, and a few good games.

Roger Ebert's review of the movie characterizes a basic truth: Sport is a vehicle for how we live life. Sport is a vehicle for ultimate human communication. Ebert, as well as that final scene in *Field of Dreams* where Ray and his dad share a game of catch under the lights, confirms that some people, perhaps especially men of the male warrior archetype, don't have the words to express love, tenderness, and caring, so they use sport, or even a game of catch, to create communication.

## Special Sport Language

Sport comes equipped with a language of its own, sometimes subtle, sometimes audible, sometimes in code—or all three.

Consider, in baseball, signs from the manager or coach to a batter and signs from the catcher to the pitcher. Football players use a code to call plays; and if the quarterback chooses to change the play at the line of scrimmage, we say he is calling an audible, and even a shift in the quarterback's weight or movement of his leg sends a signal to put ends or running backs in motion. The communication between an equestrian and the horse is a shift of the reins, a squeeze of the rider's knees, or a whip to the horse's rump. Basketball teammates might signal a pass with a quick look while using a head nod or body fake to send a false message to a defending opponent. And race car officials use colored flags to communicate the start of a race, caution, one lap to go, then the paradigmatic checkered flag to signal the end of the race and its winner.

It is also interesting to note how sport transforms the meaning of words. The words *hut* and *hike* connote different messages when used by a mountain trekker versus a football quarterback under center. Thus, it is important to realize, in sport as well as in all other aspects of our lives, how we use certain words to convey meaning. Our choice of words and symbols communicate a vibratory energy force that reveals much about who we are; this is true if we are cooing to a baby, expressing a suggestion to a supervisor, speaking to neighbors at a town meeting, or rooting for our team from the sidelines. Just as when we play or sing musical notes, the way we choose to communicate determines if we generate harmony or create cacophony.

And when we realize that sport—how we play, how we cheer, and how we identify with a certain team through apparel and symbolic souvenirs—has an impact on our community, society, nation, and the world, we may find within ourselves the desire to be more aware of how much we—and many others—center our lives around sport.

## Words We Choose

In the following chapters, we'll look into some words that, when really considered, can shift our paradigms and take us deeper on our journey into the games, exposing the joy, the meaning, and the purpose behind it all. We may find that the language we choose to use is a reflection of old, ingrained cultural paradigms. But with greater awareness of our sportual inner self, we can shift our real thoughts about the meaning of our sporting pursuits. Or, as Einstein said, "No problem can be solved from the same level of consciousness that created it."

Often, the significant problems we face originate from the stories we feed ourselves or that others have fed us. Those stories, obviously, are comprised of words. But what are words? Nothing but symbols for thought—thoughts that we can step away from, if we choose. In *Spontaneous Evolution*, authors Steve Bhaerman and Bruce Lipton conveyed this concept when they wrote: "Most importantly, by stepping outside of our stories, we can see that stories are, well, merely stories, no more real than words on a restaurant menu are edible. However, the meaning we bring to those words usually determines what we end up eating."[19]

Just as a bounty of food might be brought to our table at a restaurant, often certain words come to us from others in a manner that can only be described as grace, a divine or inspirational gift. Or as Marianne Williamson reminds us in her *Morning Meditation,* "A path lies before you . . . a path of perfect grace."[20] While composing this chapter, I received the gift of grace through an email message from Madisyn Taylor, writing in *Daily OM*, about the energy of words, which, she says, "are not abstract, disconnected entities used only to convey meaning; they are powerful transmitters of feeling.... Words carry energy and this gives language its power and its potential to heal or hurt."[21]

Taylor writes: "Most of us can remember a time that someone sent a word our way and it stuck with us. It may have been the first time we received a truly accurate compliment or the time a friend or sibling called us a name, but either way it stuck. This experience reminds us that what we say has weight and power and that being conscious means being aware of how we use words."[22]

Taylor suggests that we monitor how the words we say and hear affect our body and emotions, and how the words we speak seem to affect others. She notes that words spoken quickly carry less power than words spoken slowly and with confidence. And when we listen carefully to others, we also tend to center ourselves before speaking, thus giving our words greater integrity. Taylor concludes that when "we truly begin to harness the power of speech . . . our words can be intelligent messengers of healing and light, transmitting deep and positive feelings to those who receive them."[23]

Think about that the next time you become angry at a fan, wearing the opposing team's jersey, who spills beer on your lap or when you are tempted to curse at someone on the roadway or in a social setting.

When we pay attention to our words, we realize how they shape our thinking and that it's our thought process that creates much of our experience. Consider the following words with detrimental meaning that are used commonly and often without a second thought in all kinds of sport: kill, sudden death, draw blood, suicide, knock out, spike, shoot, strike, hit, sack, whip, spear (spearing with helmets in football).

George Carlin comically heightens our awareness of words with his comparison of baseball and football:

> I enjoy comparing baseball and football:
>
> Baseball is a nineteenth-century pastoral game. Football is a twentieth-century technological struggle.

Baseball is played on a diamond, in a park. The baseball park! Football is played on a gridiron, in a stadium, sometimes called Soldier Field or War Memorial Stadium.

Baseball begins in the spring, the season of new life. Football begins in the fall, when everything's dying.

In football you wear a helmet. In baseball you wear a cap.

Football is concerned with downs—what down is it? Baseball is concerned with ups—who's up?

In football you receive a penalty. In baseball you make an error.

In football the specialist comes in to kick. In baseball the specialist comes in to relieve somebody.

Football has hitting, clipping, spearing, piling on, personal fouls, late hitting, and unnecessary roughness. Baseball has the sacrifice.

Football is played in any kind of weather: rain, snow, sleet, hail, fog. In baseball, if it rains, we don't go out to play.

Baseball has the seventh-inning stretch. Football has the two-minute warning.

Baseball has no time limit: we don't know when it's gonna end—might have extra innings. Football is rigidly timed, and it will end even if we've got to go to sudden death.

In baseball, during the game, in the stands, there's kind of a picnic feeling; emotions may run high or low, but there's not too much unpleasantness. In football, during the game in the stands, you can be sure that at least twenty-seven times you're capable of taking the life of a fellow human being.

And finally, the objectives of the two games are completely different:

In football the object is for the quarterback, also known as the field general, to be on target with his aerial assault, riddling the defense by hitting his receivers with deadly accuracy in spite of the blitz, even if he has to use shotgun. With short bullet passes and long bombs, he marches his troops into enemy territory, balancing this aerial assault with a sustained ground attack that punches holes in the forward wall of the enemy's defensive line.

In baseball the object is to go home! And to be safe!—I hope I'll be safe at home![24]

# Media Influence

The broadcast media is a primary mechanism for mass communication in the world, both in nations where the World Wide Web is readily available and where it is not. But even before the technological developments gave us radio and television, devious minds found ways to lead the masses to their particular points of view.

Consider, for example, the famous testimony by Nazi leader Herman Goering at the Nuremberg trials about the German government's ability to manipulate the populace by programming them with fear: "Naturally the common people don't want war. . . . But, after all, it is the leaders of the country who determine the policy, and it is always a simple matter to drag the people along, whether it is a democracy, or a fascist dictatorship, or a parliament, or a communist dictatorship. . . . All you have to do is tell them they are being attacked, and denounce the peacemakers for lack of patriotism and exposing the country to danger. It works the same in any country."[25]

At various levels, the media hypes a similarity between sport and war: communities have cross-town rivalries and major universities are touted as being in a civil war. But what is war but the ultimate human struggle over conflicting paradigms or belief systems? In war, men and women fight to the death, they risk their very lives for an ideal that has been mentally and emotionally imposed by a government or combative leader through the best media mechanism of the day: Internet, talk radio, radio, television, movies and newsreels, newspapers and magazines, pamphlets possibly dropped from airplanes, war bond campaigns, loud speakers, megaphones, citizen rallies, religious pulpits, parades with drum and bugle corps, word of mouth, tribal war drums, whispered secrets, and even the recognition and prestige of being a soldier in uniform.

Could sport, with its hype either on local or national media, be a practice ground for war? We have definitely created a link between sport and war in this country. A war between East and West, North and South, right and wrong, us and them, Republicans and Democrats so that even divisiveness within our political system threatens a primary tenet of our Pledge of Allegiance: that we be "one nation, under God, indivisible, with liberty and justice for all."

Where is the peace in a society and media that promotes separation? Where is the common sense in communication that advocates labeling? Where is our inclusive indivisibility, our sense of "liberty and justice for all," in a nation where politicians, with the help of the media, resort to name-calling, which is really verbal bullying, especially during election campaigns? And how much of that paradigm is fostered in media-promoted heckling of "the others"—either the other point of view, the other candidate, the other religion, or the other team?

In the aspects of sport that I love, there is no room for war-like sentiment or language. And this non-dualistic attitude is also common among most of the coaches and players I know, especially at the small-college level. As Steve Bhaerman and Bruce Lipton state in *Spontaneous Evolution,* we can avoid hostility and war-like thinking "By making the unconscious conscious. When we recognize we can be programmed by fear, we are less susceptible to manipulations by those who benefit from mass conflict."[26]

# Creating Positive Language

Because the mind doesn't comprehend the concept of *not* when you say, "Don't do this," or "Don't do that," I remind my team to create positive sentences and to avoid the words do not or don't in their vocabulary. The words create the thought that creates the reality that brings into existence the thing you don't want to happen—or fulfillment of what you want to avoid.

Language is an extension of our thoughts, which is why negative language—and how to avoid using it—is often a discussion within my team. One of the phrases I often hear during a time-out or between games is "don't let up." This statement implies that we *can* let up. Similarly, when a player says to a server "don't serve out," the last words the server hears is "serve out"—which is the last thing I want on my server's mind.

This concept is easy to communicate with others. When you hear, "Don't think of the Statue of Liberty," or "Don't think of a pink elephant with green rabbit ears," what do you think about? What are you thinking about right now? Or try saying this, "Don't think of slicing a lemon." Salivating yet?

The imagery in words is powerful. Imagery builds thoughts; thoughts shape perception; perception creates action. We create this on my team with "terminating the play" instead of "killing" the ball. Instead of running "suicides" for sprinting, we run ladders, which is the same exercise with a different name. Osho, the Indian mystic and spiritual teacher, makes the same observation between perception and reality. We can locate joy within the games if we focus on the positive language over the negative:

> *Once you have started seeing the beauty of life,*
> *ugliness starts disappearing.*
> *If you start looking at life with joy,*
> *sadness starts disappearing.*
> *You cannot have heaven and hell together,*
> *you can have only one.*
> *It is your choice.*

That said, it is your choice to look deeply into these following chapters, each of which explores a different meaning for some of the more frequently used words in sport. You can choose heaven or hell. It is my hope that you find heaven—that is, the joy in these games we play.

Box Score:

What are your favorite words? What words do you say most often in coaching, parenting, and/or playing? If you reconsider those words from their origins, do they take on a new, more conscious meaning? Pay attention to how your body feels and how you feel about yourself when you choose positive language or negative language.

# Spirit
## "to breathe"
## (purpose of life)

**Spir-it (spir-et)**

*noun:*

an animating or vital principle held to give life to physical organisms; a supernatural being or essence: Holy Spirit; the immaterial intelligent or sentient part of a person; a lively or brisk quality in a person or a person's actions; a person having a character or disposition of a specified nature[27]

*Dum spiro, spero. (While I breathe, I hope.)*

—Cicero

*Spiritual relationship is far more precious than physical. Physical relationship divorced from spiritual is body without soul.*

—Mohandas Gandhi

# Redefining the Word

This word *spirit* gets around. It's as popular—and necessary—as breathing. Consider the etymology from the Latin: *spiritus*, "to breathe;" *spirare*, "to blow or breathe."

To inspire literally means "to breathe in." To inspire is necessary. Without breath, we do not live. This is an ancient truth. The Bible tells us: "The Lord God formed man out of the clay of the ground and blew into his nostrils the breath of life, and so man became a living being."[28]

Inspiration gives us meaning and purpose. Inspiration, whether from a coach or fans or an athlete's internal spirit, inspires teams. When we—whether as individuals or players on a team—experience that which inspires us, we breathe it in and it becomes us; literally, the molecules of oxygen become our cells and feed our brain, our muscles, our very being.

The intent behind an inspired action determines its sometimes unconscious, but certain, outcome. We say that the prevailing athlete or athletes have the greater spirit, the stronger drive, the will to prevail. And the depth of that spirit can determine the difference between a strikeout or a home run, a touchdown or a goal-line stand, a powerful spike or a blocked shot, the winning goal or a great save.

## Inspired by the ESPY Award

Sport has become increasingly analyzed and mechanistic, often removing spirit from the game for both participants and observers. Instead, let's imagine sport as a living, breathing being, infused with spirit, and realize sport is an active participant in the ongoing process of human evolution, not a victim of that evolution.

Consider, for example, the ESPY award for "Best Moment" where we are renewed and inspired by players who breathe new life into our games. A personal favorite is when Central Washington University softball players Mallory Holtman and Liz Wallace took home ESPN's ESPY award for the year's best moment.[29] If you're a regular ESPN viewer, you will have already heard about Holtman and Wallace's inspirational contribution to sport in April 2009. If this story is new to you, take a breath and prepare to be emotionally inspired.[30]

In a home game on Senior Day for Central Washington University against Western Oregon, Western Oregon's outfielder, Sara Tucholsky, hit her first-ever career home run, a three-run shot in the top of the second. However, when tagging first base, Tucholsky tore her ACL and fell after rounding the base, unable to continue around the base path.

The incident is similar to what Dawn Todd experienced, as described earlier in the Warm-Up section of this book. But there is a big difference. Dawn was already a runner on base and was tagged out after she fell between first and second base. Had she made it to second, she could have been replaced with a pinch runner without penalty to the team. But according to the rules of collegiate softball, inserting a pinch runner for Sara would diminish her home run to a single—the point to which she was able to advance on her own—and the runners ahead of her would be allowed to advance only one base and not score. If Jimmy Buffett were there, he would call upon the lyrical wisdom of one of his songs that I use on a regular basis: "Someone call a decent physician!" Or call for some other greater—inspirational—power. Well, maybe Holtman and Wallace heard that higher call.

With Tucholsky's teammates forbidden to aid her because of the rule that a player on the same team as the runner cannot help the runner, she was ready to settle for a single and a pinch runner when Holtman and Wallace stepped forward. They created a chair with their arms, as is taught in first-aid classes, and lifted her off the ground. (Rules permit this because defensive players are in the field of play and are allowed to touch a base runner.) The small crowd watched as the two CWU players carried Tucholsky to second, lowering her so that her foot touched the base, then doing the same at third and home, thus voluntarily helping her complete her first home run and the final play of her collegiate career.

This sequence was captured on a home video camera by a spectator in the stands and was featured on ESPN's *Sportscenter* where it gained national recognition.[31] Holtman and Wallace were later interviewed on CBS' *The Early Show, ESPN First Take,* and *The Ellen DeGeneres Show.*[32]

*According to the rules,* Central Washington University could have won the game, and Tucholsky, who hit the home run, would have been held to a single. But, *sportually,* CWU elevated themselves above that of a mere opponent and victor. With one unselfish act of kindness, they inspired all who observed, which, thanks to ESPN and the Internet, turned out to be literally the world. And we can only wonder how Mallory Holtman and CWU's Liz Wallace will further inspire others as they relate this story to friends, peers, and even their future children.

## Living and Breathing Sport

Is it possible to have too much of a good thing? If the good thing—even sport—no longer inspires, then, yes, I think it is. Is that happening as sport becomes over-analyzed and mechanistic? Is profit and hype removing spirit—and joy—from the game?

Do you remember when professional football was played only on Sunday? Then came Monday Night Football and the annual Detroit Lions game on Thanksgiving. Then other teams began to play on Turkey Day too. Now, we have weekly Thursday Night Football. Why not play at least one football game every night of the week?

Do you remember when the Major League Baseball season was 154 games and ended in September with the World Series in October? Now with the elimination of doubleheaders, the 162-game schedule seems longer and the expanded playoff format puts the World Series well into late October and early November.

Do you remember when the NCAA Basketball Tournament comprised eight teams? Then it was expanded to sixteen, thirty-two, forty-eight, sixty-four, and sixty-eight teams. Now, there's talk of expanding the number of teams even further, and a multi-round NCAA football championship series remains a possibility.

How far can athletic seasons be expanded? As far as media advertising dollars, owners' desire to put meat in the seats, and fan interest will go, I suppose.

Consider, for example, the cynical view that would *require* every team of every sport at every level, from collegiate to professional, to play a game every day. The result would be a world of sport that would go on, literally, 24/7/365—almost. The only competition-free day would be New Year's Day when no game would be played but a television extravaganza (greater than the Super Bowl) would be the setting for crowning the Grand Champion of All Sport. But to earn that honor, the award-winning team would have had to maintain the highest interest of fans for the entire preceding 364 days. Is it possible to maintain that level of both saturation and interest? Personally, I think not. But before we rule out the possibility, we would be wise to do a spirit check with the advertisers, the owners, and the glassy-eyed fans.

## Spirit Guides

Inspiration, rooted in sport, can carry over into other realms. I, too, became inspired while writing these pages when two deer appeared less than twenty feet away from me in my backyard. This prompted me to look up "deer as spirit guides" on the Internet and here is part of what I found:

> *Deer's Wisdom includes:*
> *Gentleness in word, thought and touch,*
> *Ability to listen,*
> *Grace and appreciation for the beauty of balance,*
> *Understanding of what's necessary for survival,*
> *Power of gratitude and giving,*
> *Ability to sacrifice for the higher good,*
> *Connection to the woodland goddess,*
> *Alternative paths to a goal.*[33]

And

> *If a deer appears to you, she may teach you to be alert yet innocent, to cause no harm to any other living thing, even*

*in thought. All too often, our illnesses are perpetuated by negative thoughts and emotions that become encrusted in our spiritual layers. Clearing is necessary: clearing of body, mind, heart, and spirit to rid yourself of these burdens.*[34]

Perhaps the Milwaukee Bucks are on to something!

## Team Breath

In December 2008, I had the opportunity to sit in on a convention session with former Nebraska volleyball coach Terry Pettit who asked us to consider the verb *to conspire*. Terry, who had studied writing and poetry in his undergraduate years and is a great teller of sport stories, has a magical way of weaving words and meaning. He pointed out that the current corrupted definition of conspire is to secretly plot an unlawful act or to participate in a conspiracy. Then, he told us that conspire comes from the Latin *con*, which means "with" and, as we've already seen, *spiro*, "to breathe." The real meaning, then, is "to breathe together."

He said the word again, a bit softer, as though it were the sound of a deer emerging from a woods and appearing in a glen. He spoke so softly that we all had to lean toward him to hear: "to *breathe* together." In that moment, it became clear to me that the word conspire and its cousin conspiracy have been misconstrued and contorted with a negative connotation of crime and deceit; yet *breathing together* defines what we do as a team.

Pettit then performed his poem "After the Loss" to help us see the physical manifestation of our spiritual purpose as coaches, weaving a tapestry of sport and spirituality that enables our teams to co-create sportuality:

*They consider my voice*
*An inappropriate companion*
*To the pounding of their blood,*
*Hot with fatigue and disappointment.*
*Their heads are bent*

*Like a ficus toward the light,*
*But there is no light.*
*Instead they wait*
*For the practiced words*
*That huddle in my brain,*
*Pocket change from losing.*
*And I know that I cannot reach*
*Them with words.*
*And so we breathe in silence,*
*A conspiracy of players and coaches*
*Reassured by the rhythmic heaving*
*Of spent muscle, flesh and synapse.*
*Each letting go reminds us:*
*We were prepared.*
*There was opportunity.*
*We could have won.*
*These unspoken truths are*
*What we take with us.*
*That, and this solitude,*
*This beautiful, tired breathing.*[35]

Now, with that perspective and understanding, consider the image of two football teams lined up in the winter cold, their breath visible to the naked eye. Would you consider the players guilty of a conspiracy, of preparing to do wrong? No, they are conspiring—breathing together—to perform to their greatest ability: to advance the ball through offense or to hold the line or take the ball through defense. Together, the teams—seemingly opponents—are working together to play the game they love, to entertain the fans, to express their athleticism. This is sport. It is conspiracy in the highest definition of the word.

Team spirit, literally, is team breath. When we reflect on "the great team we have," we mean that "our team members all live for the greater good of the team." And when we adopt that meaning, we go beyond our egos to a belief in something greater than ourselves. We go beyond thinking of the handful of players on the court or the field to thinking about the whole of humanity.

# The Spirit of Sport in World Leadership

My favorite article about the essence of President Barack Obama can be found in, of all places, the January 20, 2009, issue of *Sports Illustrated*, which appeared on the newsstands only a few days before he took office. The article, "The Audacity of Hoops," written by longtime *SI* staff writer Alexander Wolff, is a piece of reporting and analysis that mixes personal and national history, psychology, sociology, geography, politics, and, yes, sports. In the process, Wolff has shown how Obama has introduced sport, in particular, basketball, into the realm of world leadership.

Wolff's article states that Obama and his campaign team played a game of basketball on all of the primary caucus and election days, except one, in New Hampshire where Obama lost the primary. People took notice of how this presidential candidate mixed sport and politics. The campaign for Republican candidate, John McCain, as Wolff reports, "aired an attack ad suggesting that Obama had disrespected the troops by shooting hoops with them, with footage of his three-pointer in Kuwait." The National Basketball Association offered to help install an indoor full court at the White House to replace the current outdoor half court. Washington Wizards owner Abe Pollin offered Obama the use of the Verizon Center. And his staff envisioned that he would play often on the court at Camp David.

But Obama's love of basketball is not just about basketball. It's not just about sport. It's also about world leadership. Wolff's article points out that basketball might influence the way Obama governs. He writes, "People it will behoove him to get along with—both Sen. John Thune (R., SD) and Spanish Prime Minister José Luis Rodríguez Zapatero play regularly—could wind up as guests in Presidential games. For Cabinet officials there will be face time with the President, and for those who play (prospective Education Secretary Arne Duncan, Attorney General-designate Eric Holder) there will be in-your-face time as well." [36]

In this way, Obama uses basketball to connect. And isn't connection—regardless of the danger or regardless of the circumstances, when the game is on the line—the very essence, the very spirit, the very breath of both sport and politics? In *Dreams from*

*My Father,* Obama's 1995 memoir, he writes about "a way of being together when the game was tight and the sweat broke and the best players stopped worrying about their points and the worst players got swept up in the moment and the score only mattered because that's how you sustained the trance. In the middle of which you might make a move or a pass that surprised even you, so that even the guy guarding you had to smile, as if to say, 'Damn . . .' "[37]

In sport, there is balance, too: an equilibrium. Unlike in war where armies consist of whatever number of soldiers they can recruit, enlist, draft, or enslave, sport teams play with the same number of players (except in some sports, like hockey, where parental referees sometime tell penalized players to take a "time-out" for undue roughness while the rest of the team plays shorthanded). Sports games last for a regulated amount of time: forty-five minutes, sixty minutes, or, in baseball, whenever one team wins. Or as Yogi Berra used to say, "It ain't over till it's over."

Wolff reports on how Obama brings this balance to the stage of world politics, perhaps, hopefully, setting a positive example for other world leaders who would rather play by the unruly rule of "strength in numbers." Wolff writes: "Throughout Obama's career there's been a pattern of counterweight, of his providing yin where there's yang, and vice versa. At Punahou (Hawaii, where Obama played high school basketball), with order and orthodoxy all around, he chose to develop a gut-bucket game. On Chicago's South Side, where hoops and life tend toward entropy, he worked as an organizer. At Harvard Law School, roiled by ideological polarization, he was the difference-splitter. Basketball's appeal, Obama told HBO's Bryant Gumbel last year, lies in an 'improvisation within a discipline that I find very powerful.' With its serial returns to equilibrium—cut backdoor against an overplay; shoot when the defense sags—the game represents Obama's intellectual nature come alive."[38]

The inherent balance, the essence of sport (as well as in all of Nature), is, as Wolff writes, "as old as the ancients."[39] And this necessary equilibrium also applies to the balance between rights of the individual and the welfare of the group. In his article, Wolff quotes Obama's words in *Audacity of Hope,* "Our individualism has always been bound by a set of communal values, "the glue upon which every healthy society depends."[40]

Wolff elaborates:

> In the Africa of his roots he (Obama) sees the pendulum swung so far toward the collective that the individual can be overburdened and paralyzed. In the America he's poised to lead he sees individuals gaming a financial system so enfeebled that the collective faces deficits and recession. Where is the golden mean, that place where We the People might find "a way of being together," where the best players stop worrying about their points and the worst players get swept up in the moment and the score only matters because that's how you sustain the trance?
>
> The same tension sits at the heart of hoops. Titles await teams that can braid what Obama, speaking of America here, has called "these twin strands—the individualistic and the communal, autonomy and solidarity." Maybe Barry O'Bomber needed to be a Punahou reserve to become a Hawaii state champion. Maybe Barack Obama needed to be a community organizer to become a U.S. Senator. And maybe, just maybe, Americans chose him as their next president because they too have come to recognize that in the end it's not about you, it's about the team.[41]

Regardless of your political persuasion and regardless of whether you are a sport fan or not, Obama's appearance in the White House is like a new coach coming into a team. He's a coach with a different paradigm. There are those who don't like him because of that. But then many people don't like change simply because it's . . . well, change. But whether you buy into Obama as president and as this era's new coach, it is possible he speaks for the spirit, the hope, the future of the world.

# The Essence of Spirit

Is there nothing greater than instilling team spirit among millions of people and then "competing"—that is, *working with* other groups of millions of people—to improve and, indeed, find joy in the shared life on Earth, a renewed, aware, and peaceful Earth?

In his song, "Only Time Will Tell," Jimmy Buffett asks us to consider: "Are we destined to be ruled by a bunch of old white men, who compare the world to football and a program to defend?" If that is our view of the world, collectively we participate in war mentality, territorialism, domination, and defensiveness that lead to wars, death, and destruction.

Mohandas Gandhi said, "A nation's culture resides in the hearts and in the soul of its people." Likewise, our sport reflects our cultural values and beliefs. Where we put our energy and how we get our energy is also reflected in the games we play, the attention we give them, and the economic and social impact they have on our culture. Do we engage in us-versus-them turf wars? Or do we participate and cooperate as co-conspirators for a healthy planetary population?

For example, prior to the start of the NCAA football season in 2009, the NCAA and the AFCA (American Football Coaches Association) created "RESPECT Weekend" to be held during the opening game of the season. Following is the press release from the NCAA:

Tuesday, September 1, 2009

INDIANAPOLIS—The American Football Coaches Association (AFCA) and the NCAA are partnering on a national sportsmanship initiative called "RESPECT Weekend," which is set to begin with the Sept. 3-7 weekend of the college football season.

The AFCA and NCAA are encouraging all college football teams to meet at midfield before the kickoff of each game for a pregame handshake. The two head coaches and the two directors of athletics (or a representative of the athletics department) are to lead the sportsmanship gesture.

"This is a symbolic initiative that says to the football world, our fans, our students, our student-athletes and athletics departments that sportsmanship is a vital part of the successful football programs we have in this country," said AFCA Executive Director Grant Teaff. "We wanted to show sportsmanship in a clear way."

Television viewers and those attending the games will see signs in stadiums promoting the theme. Video public service announcements, public address scripts and merchandise giveaways also are part of RESPECT Weekend.

The AFCA code of conduct already calls for coaches to shake hands before and after each game. This initiative is being conducted to help reinforce that philosophy.

"We think it is important for coaches to shake hands after the game win or lose to show true sportsmanship and respect," Teaff said. "This is a great game that is at its pinnacle. We want to make sure we're teaching the right thing to our student-athletes, the student bodies and the youngsters out there watching the game."

All NCAA institutions have been encouraged to participate, but the campaign is not mandatory.

The initiative stems from a two-year NCAA research study of student-athletes, coaches, conference commissioners, administrators and fans that indicated fan behavior was the most pressing matter to be addressed at college sporting events.[42]

While some may have found this initiative refreshing, others took time to find everything wrong about it. In response to an online poll by ESPN asking fan thoughts about the establishment of such a handshake before the first game of the season, the following comments and several others of a similar nature appeared on the website www. sports.espn.go.com on August 15, 2009, even prior to the NCAA's media release.

> "The players don't like this crap, coaches don't like it, fans don't like it. I am SO sick and tired of the NCAA, NFL, etc. trying to sissify what is supposed to be a violent, aggressive game."

> "What the hell! This is football. What's next . . . are they going to hug and kiss before they knock the crap out of each other? Have they seen what happens when Michigan and Ohio State meet at midfield before a game? That is the way it should be before a game. The two teams should be prepared for war not love!!! Save the handshake for soccer, basketball, and tennis. Who the hell would shake hands before a fist fight? DUMB!"

> "Giving your opponents a handshake is not a sign of respect when it's forced on you. This whole concept just reflects the continued attempts to feminize men in this country. Eventually our genetics are going to rebel.!!!!!"[43]

The bad news is that our genetics, the DNA that unites all of us, *are* rebelling. War-based thinking, depletion/pollution of natural resources, extinction of species, and rampant diseases such as obesity, cancer, heart disease, diabetes, alcoholism, and addictions are the symptoms. It is costing us trillions to fight wars, create a system of health care, manage addictions, and clean up our messes. We're definitely missing the spiritual piece of the equation with the kind of thinking expressed by the rabid fans at the end of the NCAA blog.

After all, individuals in other sports honor each other pre-contest: Boxers touch gloves; jousters salute; baseball players stand on the baselines and remove their caps for the national anthem; volleyball players shake hands at the net. And of course, post-game handshakes and acknowledgements are common. It's news when coaches or players intentionally ignore the post-game handshake.

When we all can practice civility and professionalism—whether engaging in sport or engaging with each other in politics, business, or family—we will have evolved into joy and away from the influence of the multi-billion-dollar sports-media industry that breeds fan fervor with feats of superhuman fantasy.

## Mean-Spirited Media

We've reached a point where news broadcasting is becoming more like a traditional, old-paradigm sporting event. This has occurred since the advent of ESPN. We have cable channels that now politically lean to the left or lean to the right and radio talk show hosts who raise their voices to fight, fight, fight.

Major media "news" shows have largely moved away from journalism and are now considered entertainment, shaping people's thoughts, using the black/white, left/right, war-based thinking, and creating a dualistic, divisive, us-versus-them mentality.

Spirit is absent from the process, as we increasingly see broadcasters looking for an emotional audience response. For example, the 2009 NCAA football season featured the drama of quarterback Tim Tebow and coach Urban Meyer of the University of Florida. Tebow was a senior who had won the coveted Heisman Trophy as a sophomore, who enjoyed one of the greatest collegiate careers in history, and who was also an outspoken Christian. Meyer had just announced his possible retirement or at least leave due to "health concerns." While the University of Florida football team won their final game of the year, the Sugar Bowl, by a wide margin, broadcasters and cameramen alike were searching for tears, for any emotion from Tebow or Urban. "It's his last game . . . *their* last game together . . . the tears *will* come . . . ," their commentary implied, as though pleading and begging the star and the coach to comply. The post-game press conference questions focused on the emotional rather than the tactical. Why? Was it because the game story was not necessarily newsworthy? Or was this broadcasting's feeble attempt to keep viewers glued to their sets and retain ratings?

Which makes me want to ask: What holds viewer interest—emotion or e-motion (our energy in motion)?

I suggest it is our *energy* in motion: our common story, our connection within humanity, our Spirit that is within all of us—sportually.

---

**TIME-OUT:**

Regardless of your political point of view or your favorite team, listen to several radio talk show hosts speaking on political and sport issues. Pick hosts with opposing views. Consider whether they sound the same, regardless of the message. Consider whether their messages are in the spirit of divisiveness, us-versus-them, belittling opponents and those with opposing views. Is theirs the spirit in which you want to live and play?

---

# Olympic Spirit

When we consider global humanity, the International Olympic Committee (IOC) and the Olympic games naturally come to mind. The IOC is one of very few global institutions that exist on the planet, and the Olympic Games are the only global competitions that involve all recognized sports in one venue, winter and summer. Thus, the Olympics are an inspiration, as well as an event, that brings the world together. As President Obama stated at a presentation to the IOC on

October 2, 2009, "[We] reach for a dream—a dream that no matter who we are, where we come from; no matter what we look like or what hand life has dealt us; with hard work and discipline and dedication, we can make it if we try. That's not just the American dream. That is the Olympic Spirit. It's the essence of the Olympic Spirit."[44]

The Olympic spirit is one of friendship, fair play, peace, honour, and glory[45]—to inspire and motivate youth to be the best they can be. In that spirit of fair play, after commenting on the powerful influence of mean-spirited media above, it's also important to recognize the global media for doing an excellent job of bringing the games and the IOC principles to the world. Yes, nationalism does drive each nation to "go for the gold" and bring home as many medals as possible, but there is also a great global pride in the Olympics' *inter*national spirit that motivates us to cheer for all the champions, regardless of the nation they represent. In the Olympics, sport is pure, athletes play on a level field, competition lives up to its original definition of working with (not against), and the media simply reports.

In the Olympics, where the athletes are world class yet still (ideally) amateurs, more than in any other sport venue, anything can happen. Consider, for example, the unlikely entry of a bobsled team from the tropical island of Jamaica in the cold-weather 1988 Winter Olympics in Calgary, Alberta, Canada.

Because bobsledders start a run down the icy shoot by sprinting, Jamaica first attempted to enlist runners, but the island nation's many sprinters weren't interested, so the military got involved. The original team consisted of the unlikely combination of an army lieutenant, an air force captain, a national reserve private, and a railway engineer. And they were coached by an American.

The team, as ultimate underdogs, immediately became fan favorites. Because they had very little practice on a bobsled track, they borrowed sleds from other countries. In the true Olympic spirit, the cold-weather athletes also offered guidance and support.

During one of their four runs down the course, the team lost control of their sled, slid to a stop, and didn't officially finish the race. In a touching scene, they carried their crashed sled to the finish line amidst applause and cheers from the spectators along the sidelines.[46]

They competed again in the 1992 Winter Olympics and qualified for the 1994 Winter Olympics where they stunningly finished in fourteenth place, ahead of the United States, Russia, Australia, France, and Italy. In 2000, they won a gold medal at the World Push Championships in Monaco, but failed to qualify for the Winter Olympics in 2006 and 2010. They were the source of inspiration for a major motion picture, *Cool Runnings,* the storyline of which loosely follows their exploits.

This willingness of the Jamaicans to embrace cold weather sports is *sportual*: stretching climatic boundaries and perceived limitations toward inclusion of the literally polar opposite and testing their spirits within the physical constructs of world competition.

## The Spirit of Baseball

As associate chaplain and a physical educator at Kalamazoo College, I felt called to connect the physical and spiritual and to share this with my campus community. So in January 2002, I traveled to Indianapolis, Indiana, to attend a conference on joy hosted by the Association for Humanistic Psychology. I believed that if I were going to help faculty and students find their joy, I should have a greater idea of how the process actually works.

Well, of course, what the conference revealed was that I already *knew* how to access my joy . . . through baseball. Yes, baseball. Just like James Earl Jones, as Terrance Mann in *Field of Dreams,* left us with that ageless, timeless thought:

> Ray, people will come, Ray. They'll come to Iowa for reasons they can't even fathom. They'll turn up your driveway not knowing for sure why they're doing it. They'll arrive at your door as innocent as children, longing for the past. 'Of course, we won't mind if you look around,' you'll say. It's only $20 per person. They'll pass over the money without even thinking about it: for it is money they have and peace they lack.

> And they'll walk out to the bleachers; sit in shirtsleeves on a perfect afternoon. They'll find they have reserved

seats somewhere along one of the baselines, where they sat when they were children and cheered their heroes. And they'll watch the game, and it'll be as if they dipped themselves in magic waters. The memories will be so thick they'll have to brush them away from their faces.

People will come, Ray. The one constant through all the years, Ray, has been baseball. America has rolled by like an army of steamrollers. It has been erased like a blackboard, rebuilt, and erased again. But baseball has marked the time. This field, this game: it's a part of our past, Ray. It reminds us of all that once was good and it could be again.

Oh ... people will come, Ray. People will most definitely come.

The materials for the conference included a list of several seminars, including one-hour presentations by some very joyous people who were also very serious seekers. There were many topics to choose from, but—Hey! Lo and behold!—there was one on the spirituality of baseball! I chose baseball!

The presenter was Steve Bhaerman, one of the headline keynote speakers, who usually performs as his comedian alter-ego Swami Beyondananda. (Note: *ananda* in Sanskrit means "joy or bliss," which means that Swami Beyondananda is "beyond joy." How cool is that?) But in this particular session, he was simply Steve, a regular guy who also loves baseball.

Steve shared his story of growing up in Brooklyn, being a normal boy with normal boyhood exploits. Then he talked about baseball, and he said something I will never forget: "It was then that I realized baseball can be a spiritual pursuit." Read it again—out loud this time—*It was then that I realized baseball can be a spiritual pursuit.* Hello, paradigm shift.

Besides being absolutely nutty and full of puns, this guy was—and still is—a spiritual master. He was telling me that I could follow my love of sport, my passion for play, and my inborn urge to compete *and* still find enlightenment—all at the same time! What good news!

But the "aha" moments kept coming: You mean all those hours I invested in the gym had a purpose? You mean my sons' pursuit of baseball was actually shaping their souls? Hallelujah!

Less than ten years later, Steve would coauthor a major paradigm-shifting book titled *Spontaneous Evolution* (Hay House, 2009) that goes well beyond sport and into the realm of evolution and the state of humanity, ultimately conveying the message that we are all one, that we all sink or swim together. This book, written along with Bruce Lipton, author of *Biology of Belief,* is a work I highly recommend if we are to evolve anything, including sport.

Baseball has come increasingly into our cultural awareness, having been a part of our story for well over a century. In fact, in Ken Burns' documentary *Baseball*, he says: "Baseball is the only sport that has accompanied the entire narration of the United States" from its agrarian roots to industry and now the information age; through wars, civil rights and women's rights, depression and abundance. Mass media has embraced it as "America's pastime." We now have the MLB television network that replays games from all decades 24/7. Major leagues have expanded, and almost every mid-size city has a minor league team that offers great performances by young, enthusiastic athletes who are every bit as entertaining as the guys in the majors. The great American pastime has come back yet again to inspire yet another generation.

While some may consider baseball to be boring, it actually brings a calmer, more peaceful, more civil way of life. Consider all of its intricacies and moves, strategies and finesses that those very familiar with the game relish. Recall all the great baseball movies: *A League of Their Own, Field of Dreams, The Natural, Pride of the Yankees, Angels in the Outfield, Major League, Bull Durham, Bang the Drum Slowly, Fever Pitch.* And, then, you realize these are not just cinemagraphic tales of sport. Rather, each portrays the finer qualities of life, elements the Bible calls "fruits of the spirit:" love, joy, peace, patience, kindness, goodness, faithfulness, gentleness, self-control.[47]

Several spiritual masters have said it is imperative that we infuse spirit into the games we play in order to fully experience their fruits. Yes, even including the contact sports such as football, hockey, and rugby. In fact, one of the more spiritual moments of Super Bowl XLIV in 2010 occurred after the game when New Orleans Saints quarterback Drew Brees held his young son in the midst of the on-field celebration, sharing the miracle for that city with his own personal miracle.

## Spirit and Spirituality

After presenting the origins of and meaning in the great religions in his book, *The Mystic Heart: Discovering a Universal Spirituality in the World's Religions*, Wayne Teasdale continues with the following observation: "By allowing inward change, while at the same time simplifying our external life, spirituality serves as our greatest single resource for changing our centuries-old trajectory of violence and division. Spirituality is profoundly transformative when it inspires in us the attitude of surrender to the mystery in which we live, move and have our being."[48]

In discussing sportuality, can we find our points of transformation within this arena of competition with others and with ourselves, thus transforming our thoughts about violence and division? That we can move away from this division toward the peace promised by all religions is, I believe, why we should continue to explore this intersection of sport and spirit.

Patsy Neal did this in her book *Sport and Identity*:

> There are moments of glory that go beyond the human expectation, beyond the physical and emotional ability of the individual. Something unexplainable takes over and breathes life into the known life. One stands on the threshold of miracles that one cannot create voluntarily.... Call it a state of grace, or an act of faith ... or an act of God. It is there, and the impossible becomes possible.... The athlete goes beyond herself; she transcends the natural. She touches a piece of heaven and becomes the recipient of power from an unknown source.

The power goes beyond that which can be defined as physical or mental. The performance almost becomes a holy place—where a spiritual awakening seems to take place. The individual becomes swept up in the action around her—she almost floats through the performance, drawing on forces she has never previously been aware of.[49]

These forces, dear reader, are sportual forces. They are spirituality and sport fusing into *one*.

# The Spirit of Sport in Movies

The movies mentioned previously appear to be about sport but are really about the spirit, the essence, of life. The same can be said of the movie *The Sandlot*. This flick tells us a lot about searching for our true spirit inside in order to overcome fear, which can also lurk inside.

The storyline is that of a new kid on the block being accepted as the ninth player on a rag-tag team who play neighborhood sandlot baseball. The nemesis to the team is a huge, ferocious, former junkyard dog, "The Beast," who resides on the other side of their leftfield fence. Local legend states that any ball hit over the fence is lost forever, for to go over the fence to retrieve it is to confront the jaws of death.

In need of a ball to continue playing one afternoon, and perhaps in an attempt to gain further acceptance by the team, the new kid, Scotty, takes his stepdad's prized baseball, which has been signed by the legendary Babe Ruth, and puts it into play. With a home run swat of his own, Scotty drives the ball over the fence, into the den of The Beast—never to be seen again. But Scotty must see it again. He must return it to his stepdad's den—before he returns from a business trip and finds it missing.

With youthful genius, the team tries five times with various inventive gadgets to retrieve the ball. Of course, none of these work. And when Scotty says, "Why don't we just knock on the door?" his friends scoff because The Beast's owner is reputed to be the meanest man in town.

Then, a spirit speaks. It is the spirit of the legendary Sultan of Swat himself who appears to Benny, the best athlete on the team, in a dream. The Babe tells Benny to "just hop over there and get it [the ball]." The Colossus of Clout affirms, "Remember, kid, there's heroes and there's legends. Heroes get remembered, but legends never die. Follow your heart, kid, and you'll never go wrong."

Benny climbs over the fence, retrieves the ball, and scales the fence to get back on the other side, the safe side—just as The Beast breaks its heavy chain, leaps the fence behind him, and gives chase. Benny shows his speed, outrunning The Beast, tearing through a town picnic then back to the sandlot, earning the nickname "The Jet," which will follow him to his major league career with the Los Angeles Dodgers.

Benny leaps over the fence, back to where the chase began. The Beast crashes through, and the fence collapses on him, pinning him to the ground. Scotty runs to the rescue, and he and Benny work together to lift the fence and free the animal, who turns on Scotty in a moment of showdown, and then slathers the boy's face with his massive tongue.

The Beast, as it turns out, is just a big jowly St. Bernard with "ball drive," the natural instinct that compels most dogs to fetch a ball or stick. Ball drive is the inherent characteristic of tracking dogs to find the subject of their search, no matter what obstacle must be overcome. And ball drive, albeit not by that name, is also found in any sport that centers around a ball. Face it, athletes of any age, even toddlers, are simply driven to throw, catch, pass, kick, or hit a ball.

Realizing the folly of fear, Scotty knocks on the door of the dog's owner, played by James Earl Jones, who says, "Why didn't you just knock on the door? I'd have gotten it for you." The message is biblical: "Knock, and it shall be opened to you."[50] The dog uncovers his treasure trove of baseballs that have been hit over the fence over the years, and the owner reveals that he is a treasure trove of baseball lore, a player destined to have been even more legendary than The Great Bambino, until hit by a pitch and blinded. "That's the way I played," he says. "One hundred percent all the time." He played with the true spirit of sport.

Giving to Scotty a ball signed by the entire 1927 Yankees team, which included the (in)famous Murderer's Row, to give to the boy's stepdad, he says, "You guys come by here and talk baseball with me, and we'll call it an even trade."

The message of overcoming fear and embracing the spirit of sport with gusto lies in more advice that Ruth, ironically also called the Titan of Terror, gives to Benny: "Everybody gets one chance to do something great. Most people don't take the chance either because they're too scared or they don't recognize it when it spits on their shoes. This is your big chance. You shouldn't let it go by."

BOX SCORE:

Consider the games you have seen, coached, or played in that remained with you either as a player, coach, spectator, or fan to shape your belief in something much greater than yourself. Have they brought you to a greater level of consciousness, to greater meaning and purpose in your life?

Who has inspired your journey in sport? Who are your spirit guides? When does your spirit leap for joy? What are your favorite sporting movies and why?

Here is The Sandlot: http://www.imdb.com/title/tt0108037/

# SECOND QUARTER:
## Competition and Community

# Competition
## "to work with"
## (peace)

---

**com-pe-ti-tion (kem-pe-'ti-shen)**

*noun (corrupted definition):*

a contest, a match; a rival[51]

**com-pete (kem-'pet)**

*verb (corrupted definition):*

to contend, vie; to strive consciously or unconsciously for an objective (as a position, profit, or prize)

*(etymological definition, Latin):*

to seek together, to come together, agree, be suitable (from *com,* which means "together" and *petere,* which means "to seek"[52]

*Persons of high self-esteem are not driven to make themselves superior to others; they do not seek to prove their value by measuring themselves against a comparative standard. Their joy is being who they are, not in being better than someone else.*

—Nathaniel Branden

*I would heartily welcome the union of East and West provided it is not based on brute force.*

—Mohandas Gandhi

During my first year of collegiate coaching, my team informed me that "we hate Team X." That moment proved to be transformational for me. In a sense, my career so far has been teaching the opposite—that we give thanks for and honor all other teams because without them there is no game.

As if in support of my belief, at the end of an HBO documentary titled *Battle for Tobacco Road: Duke vs. Carolina*, the voice-over says, "Duke and North Carolina are lucky to have each other. It's made us all better." The photos on the screen are of the teams' players shaking hands, hugging, and smiling.[53] This is a difficult concept to accept in the West, where rivalries are king and there always seems to be an enemy.

## Redefining the Word

This word *competition* demanded that I reconsider my life's work and my passion for volleyball. From the Latin *competere* "to work with" (not against), "to seek together" (not alone or only with one's tribe or team), the original meaning of this word simply turns our cultural judgment, hate, and violence-based thinking of "us against them" into somewhat of a miracle, with miracle being defined as a shift in our perception.

*Competere* . . . to work with. Say it again: to work with. *With* . . . not *against*? What do you mean they're not my/our enemy? What do you mean it's not *us* versus *them*?

Let me explain . . .

## Shifting the Competition Paradigm

Mohandas Gandhi has said, "An eye for an eye makes the whole world blind." If we consider war to be the ultimate competition (according to the current paradigm), we see that our culture has evolved—or devolved—to the point where winning and retaliation have a greater value than human relationships and even human life. It is often the idea of destructive competition that defines mainline sport here in the U.S. We have created games of dysfunction. We have made sport and war synonymous. Even the annual NCAA football contest between two intra-state rivals, Oregon and Oregon State, is called "the Civil War," a term that is an oxymoron in itself because there is nothing "civil" about war.

Steve Bhaerman and Bruce Lipton consider the idea of competition as it affects the human race and our well-being on the earth in *Spontaneous Evolution:*

> As adults of God, we now understand that healing the world comes from the inside out. Everything we do individually to become more coherent and more compassionate will reverberate in the field like ripples on a pond. Like begets like. As you sow, so shall you reap.
>
> Coherent and compassionate people have no need to dominate others, rather, they seek to empower cooperation rather than competition in everyone. Why? Because a coherent, harmonious world would be in everyone's best interest. Perhaps this is what Jesus meant by "the meek shall inherit the earth."[54]

In contrast, however, teams seem to thrive on the energy created by the current culturally accepted idea of competition. We talk about our athletes being "competitive" or we describe ourselves as "competitive," meaning we want to win—or, more likely, we hate to lose. Have you ever noticed that when "competition" or "competitive" comes up in conversation, it is usually meant as a negative? "She's so *competitive*" can mean "I really don't care for her win-at-all-costs attitude." Or, "This job is a very competitive environment" can mean "I don't want to participate in the negative energy necessary to work here."

But in reality, all competition is an opportunity for self-growth and enhancement. Again, *Spontaneous Evolution,* describing the human body, makes this very clear:

We now seem to have reached the level of complexity on this planet where seven billion human cells, operating unconsciously and using their energy at destructive cross-purposes, is no longer biologically functional.

Like the single-cell organisms that utilized environmental awareness in order to emerge into more complex and efficient organisms, human society must adopt a new paradigm of social and economic relationships. Paradoxically, this new level of cooperative awareness means maximum expression for the individual and maximum benefit for the whole. Only the seemingly impossible reconciliation of these misperceived opposites can create the emergent human that spiritual teachers tell us is our destiny.[55]

Adidas' inspirational marketing campaign featuring Muhammed Ali proclaims, "Impossible Is Nothing." This message tells us that it is possible to get to the heart and purpose of sport and realize that we can utilize true competition as a tool to reach our full, fulfilled, cooperative selves!

## Cooperative Competition

One does not play at higher levels of sport without being truly competitive. Indeed, a good, sound, tough competitor can be an inspiration, raising the bar for all involved. This would be called *cooperative competition.* And in order to win at all levels, we simply must be willing to play along, keeping the positive as our guide. Consider the potential for paradigm shifts: "She's so competitive" could become "I appreciate her work ethic and her will to make everyone around her better." And "This job is a very competitive environment" could become "Thanks to this structure and the help of my co-workers, I am able to raise the standard of my work and my outcomes. I am willing to participate to the best of my abilities as well."

Competition is actually at the root of our evolution, as Steve Bhaerman and Bruce Lipton again consider in *Spontaneous Evolution*:

> Many of our stories have been with us for millennia. But what if those supposed truths we learned about the world were wrong? What if we have it backward? What if the struggle we've been taught is natural turns out to be the most unnatural thing we could be doing? What if the social Darwinists were mistaken? What if cooperation, not competition [in the currently accepted sense], is the key to survival?[56]

Working *with* someone is so much easier and more gratifying than working *against* someone. If we become competitive in the original and literal sense of the word, we would feel gratitude instead of animosity, love instead of hate, and peace instead of war with our fellow competitors. Being *our* best allows and encourages others to be their best as well.

When a team or individual focuses energy on the other team as being "the enemy" or as something to be eliminated, we expend energy that doesn't come back. When we engage honestly in true cooperative competition, we realize our interconnectedness and we're grateful for the opportunity to raise the level of play for everyone: our teammates, the other team on the field or court, the officials, and the fans. We lift one another. The "zone" is within reach. Time stills. We feel the joy.

## God-Given Competition

When we experience the lift that comes from true competition, we realize we are not alone. As we add fans, spectators, and media to our games, sometimes we lose ourselves in the collective hype. Consider the following excerpt from the book *God-Birthing: Toward Sacredness, Personal Meaning, and Spiritual Nourishment* by Michael Dwinell in which he brings the presence of God to professional football fans:

## The NFL and God

*Today, I saw you in a thousand faces.*
  *Foxbow Stadium*
*The New England Patriots*
*versus the Houston Oilers*
  *A sell-out crowd*
*Men*
  *Men*
*Everywhere men*
  *Eating*
*Cheering*
  *Rooting*
*Drinking*
  *Especially drinking*
*Beer after beer after beer*
  *By the end of the first quarter,*
*many of the men were unsteady on their feet*
  *Eyes glazed*
*Voices louder*
  *Language cruder and cruder*
*By halftime,*
*most of the men were substantially dulled.*

  *It was unpleasant, unattractive,*
   *sometimes crude and offensive, stupid.*
*I have seen too many men that way before.*
*I had been that way too many times before.*
  *I was increasingly revolted.*
*Intelligence and awareness*
*is won at too high a price.*
  *But regardless of how revolted*
  *or offended I was,*
  *at the same time,*
  *in every face, in every pair of eyes,*
  *I saw you.*

*I saw the pain.*
  *I saw the longing.*
*I saw the beauty.*
  *I saw the vulnerability.*
*I saw your becoming,*
*pressing out and through in every face.*
  *Every face led directly to you.*

*The contest on the field*
*was really about you, wasn't it?*
  *Two teams*
*Opposing*
  *Dark and white*
*Opposite ends of the field*
  *Both striving to dominate*
*And nobody knowing the outcome*
*ahead of time*
  *And the cheering*
*The screaming*
  *The yelling*
*The booing*
  *The fanaticism is*
*Really all about you, isn't it?*
  *Cheering your awful becoming.*
*I saw a thousand faces today.*
  *Ugly and offensive*
  *and filled with your presence.*
*All that longing leads to you*
  *All that pain leads to your pain.*
*Really you were the only one there.*[57]

# Military Fanaticism

In Dwinell's poem, the teams were the sober ones, there to play the game. But somehow the fans got caught up in the fantasy of fanaticism. While this may be expected—and tolerable—within the confines of the stadium, it becomes especially problematic within the global arena when the weapons of might and destruction are technologically and militarily greater than individual strength and acumen.

Attacking or invading military generals on the ground in other countries know their purpose, but too often the general populace on the home front gets caught in military/media spinmeistering and resulting fanaticism. It happens in all countries. The symptoms are flag waving and labeling "others" as "enemy"—a non-cooperative state as debilitating as the beer-induced unsteady feet, glazed eyes, and loud voices described in Dwinell's poem.

During my life, for example, the United States has had several enemies: Japanese, Koreans, Vietnamese, Russians, Chinese, Iraqis, Iranians, Afghans. Did my government and military leaders expect me, as an American, to hate the people in those nations just because my country declared them to be an enemy? Yes, unfortunately, they did; they labeled these humans with dehumanizing names and expected me to behave with mindless reaction against them. But that is the corrupted form of competition.

## Competitive Colors

These military and governmental leaders know the value of their countries' patriotic colors: Red, white, and blue in the United States; green, white, and orange in Ireland; green, white, and red in Italy; the white field with two blue stripes and the star of David in Israel; or the red field with the hammer and sickle in Russia. What thoughts stir within you when you see the colors of your homeland? What thoughts stir within you when you see the colors of a nation that has been declared your enemy? Consider how nations have given significant meaning to those colors and have taken them onto the battlefield. Consider the role of nationalism at the Olympic Games where the countries of winning medalists are rewarded with their flags raised and their national anthems played as part of the award ceremonies.

Colors are paramount in the world of sport. One of the outward expressions of fandom is wearing the colors of one's team and even avoiding the colors of arch rivals. There are always two complementary colors: orange and black, maize and blue, green and white, red and white, scarlet and gray, maroon and gold. How do you feel when you read these words or see these colors? What images come to your mind? Do you, perhaps, also see a team mascot or logo? Do you think of a particular player or famed coach? Do you replay a great moment or performance by the team associated with those colors?

The very notion of using colors to create a competitive thought is a testament to our traditionally defined *competitive nature.*

But as fans functioning under the true meaning of competition—to seek together—then we find our *fan*-aticism in the game itself, not just blind adulation of our team. Rather than cheering for one team *over* another, we cheer for the event and the spectacle. In the Olympics, for example, yes, athletes display individual prowess and accomplishments and win medals, but it is the grandeur and the glory, the spectacle of world class amateur athletes coming together to create the Olympic Games that truly rivets our attention.

When we show our *true colors,* we want the games to win. We want our sport to survive, not divide. And when the games win, we all win. That is the ultimate competition, the true spirit of competition.

Clearly, this was the experience for those in attendance at the 2008 volleyball championship in Nebraska that I described in the Warm-Up and Ode to Joy. On that day, the fans, dressed in opposing colors, transcended rivalries, hate, and poor sportsmanship. That day, the game won.

## Competition in the Moment

Eckhart Tolle in *The Power of Now* describes the value of living in the moment for personal and spiritual growth: "Always say 'yes' to the present moment. What could be more futile, more insane, than to create inner resistance to what already is? What could be more insane than to oppose life itself, which is now and always now? Surrender to what is. Say 'yes' to life—and see how life suddenly starts working for you rather than against you."[58]

For me, being really "in the moment" occurs under two situations: when I meditate and when I play and coach volleyball. It is then when I realize that part of creating peace is *being* rather than *doing*.

Indeed, participation in sport allows, and actually demands, that we live in the moment. That is where the fans want to be. That is one reason people both play and observe sport: to exist in that perfect place of being. No past regrets, no future worries—only now. And sometimes, as George Bernard Shaw said, "The real moment of success is not apparent to the crowd." It can only be apparent to those within the game, to those feeling the joy of the competition. The crowd is watching the action; the player *is* the action.

How many times, as a fan, have we seen opponents hugging, laughing, and congratulating one another following an intense competition when we, as fans, felt like fighting? Maybe the authors of *Spontaneous Evolution* had that question in mind as they wrote, "The power of force has been in force for so long that we assume it is natural. Looking at the whole of Western history . . . we see that violence and domination have been internalized, externalized, and eternalized: violence has been declared a character of human nature for now and forever."[59]

Jesus tells us to "Love one another." Gandhi says, "Where love is, there God is also." In religious language, this is the Golden Rule. Did all the great religions intend "treat others as you would want to be treated" to apply only when not trying to win a sporting event?

Consider some of the famous rivalries: Michigan and Ohio State, Yankees and Red Sox, Jets and Sharks, North and South, East and West, Democrats and Republicans. What makes these rivalries so paramount? It is the high level of performance demanded by that competitor. When our rival is at their best, we have to be at our best. We attain our best when we begin to replace the increasingly outdated fear-based thinking with love, cooperation, and appreciation for both *their* best and *our* best. We attain our best when we excel in mind, body, and spirit and by honoring the minds, bodies, and spirits of those so-called opponents. And, reaching beyond sport, we attain our evolutionary best at the human scale when we demonstrate our increased willingness to participate in true competition—seeking together.

# The Higher Team

So, the questions arise: *Can* we remove ourselves from the outcome and not have the status of "winner" or "loser" determine our level of satisfaction and joy in the game? Can we utilize the true spirit of competition to gain, in the end, a truer sense of self?

Coaches, trainers, team owners, and the NCAA know that one cannot simply train the body to produce a great athlete. Mind, body, and spirit must be engaged to create a full, whole, healthy athlete, which is why we cannot separate the triune self and expect greatness. To that effect, French historian and founder of the modern Olympics, Pierre de Coubertin, mused, "Olympism is a doctrine of the fraternity between body and soul." And David Beard, an Australian Olympic volleyball player, reflected this idea of pure competition, "The Olympic Games should be a matter between individual athletes and the gods. Flag waving dishonors gods and men alike."

Why do athletes, especially at the Olympic level, get this concept and fans so often don't? Because fans are cajoled by hype, team colors, and media, while athletes are coached, in most cases, by integrity. Coaches emphasize teamwork, beginning with the first day of tryouts when athletes compete—come together—to make the team. Teamwork then continues as players compete—seek together—to improve themselves, each other, and, consequently, the team.

Perhaps the ultimate message of sport, as exemplified by the Olympics, is that all global citizens are all part of just *one team*, Humanity's Team. With that realization, we soon see there is always a bigger team to cheer for, a higher team to send your energy toward.

At playoff time, I find myself rooting for teams who are a part of our conference and then simply asking for an exciting game with inspired, competitive performances by all—players, coaches, and fans. Before games, we always want to know from others their opinion about who will win. What if I just want football to win, or baseball's message to be loud and clear? What if I want volleyball to prevail? What if sport wins? What if love and compassion win? What if sport leads the way toward this new—and at the same time *original*—concept of true competition?

## Replacing the Paradigm

Marianne Williamson wrote in *Illuminata*, "Winning at someone else's expense is an old paradigm and an increasingly obsolete model of success. Separation leads to disintegration and joining leads to miracles."[60] In contrast, she also wrote, "Our prayer is that our excellence might come forth and serve the world. That is power. That is success."[61]

While we seek miracles within our personal life, do we not also deeply desire the miracles so needed on Earth? I think so. I see that in myself, the athletes I coach, and the other coaches and teams with whom I interact. Yet, the further we delve into human creations of technology, the more removed we become from our origins with Nature. The more we depend upon our own creations to sustain us, the further we drift from the source of our creation, our joy, our peace. Therefore, it becomes critical that we move away from the prevailing concept of competition that promotes isolation and evolve back— literally back—toward the true spirit of competition that elevates us beyond our current state into an exhilarating joy.

Yes, this is possible. We have seen it in some of the great athletes of recent times.

In *Sacred Hoops*, Phil Jackson refers to Michael Jordan as "the epitome of the peaceful warrior." He writes, "Day in and day out, he has endured more punishment than any player in the league but he rarely shows any sign of anger."[62] This demands a significant level of sportual fortitude.

Similarly, Ken Burns, in his Emmy-award-winning documentary *Baseball*, says that when Jackie Robinson was asked by Branch Rickey to break the color barrier in baseball with the Brooklyn Dodgers in 1947, Rickey specifically told him that for two years he was forbidden to fight back against the inevitable racist words and actions.[63]

To me, it seems as if Rickey were telling Robinson to follow the philosophy of Lao Tzu who said, "If there is to be peace in the world, there must be peace in the cities. If there is to be peace in the cities, there must be peace among neighbors. If there is to be peace among neighbors, there must be peace in the family. If there is to be peace in the family, there must be peace in the heart."

In an interview with Scholastic.com in 1991, Jackie's wife, Rachel Robinson, tells us that there were some days when the racial slurs slung at Jackie Robinson challenged him greatly. On those days, he didn't have peace in his heart, and he sometimes brought that lack of peace back home to his wife.[64] Yet, he continued to act as a gentleman (gentle man) and perform as a professional athlete. He helped peace prevail in the neighborhoods of Brooklyn and within baseball itself. It was Robinson's nonviolent action that preceded Martin Luther King, Jr.'s Civil Rights Movement and, some say, paved the way for it. Indeed, Jack Roosevelt Robinson was a sportual man.

As a coach, I remind myself and tell my players that if we want to work toward world peace, our sportual and cultural pursuits need to reflect that work. In doing so, we connect with nature and human nature through our physicality and athleticism. When we enter the court or the arena expecting to win while, at the same time, honoring the presence of the other team of athletes with whom we will compete, we become like the indigenous hunters who prayed for the spirit of their prey before the hunt and at the moment of the kill. We see this ceremony performed by the Na'vi in the movie *Avatar*. In two scenes where the male lead character, Jake Sully, slays an animal with his knife, he does so with respect for the animal that will enrich his body with food. And, in that act, gains the appreciation of Neytiri, the Na'vi who showed him how to kill prey in that manner and who will eventually become his mate.

## Sharing the Other Team's Joy

But how does it feel to be the human corollary of slain prey? How does it feel to be named the "loser" in an athletic contest? One of the most difficult challenges in sport today is to teach and promote the idea of empathic joy: to refuse to compare or diminish ourselves in the presence of something beautiful, such as our own outstanding performance even when it results in a win by "the other" team.

We actually become enriched when we are able to honestly congratulate the winners and share their joy of accomplishment.

I recall a certain road game when my volleyball team was the clear favorite, but the home team played a better, more inspired match. They won in five games, with the last game being a two-point victory. As I looked at their post-game celebration, I could actually feel their joy, and I was honestly happy for them and their victory. Our team was "upset"—both in the parlance of sport when the "underdog" wins and at themselves for getting beat. But, no matter what we felt, our "sorrow" did not and could not diminish their joy. So I asked myself: How could I be feeling joy about a loss? Wasn't I supposed to be giving wisdom to my team about how, as Terry Pettit wrote in his poem "After the Loss," "We could have won." Yes, according to conventional wisdom—the accepted norm of sport—I was supposed to give wisdom. But in the deeper spirit of competition—to seek *together*—I found greater reward by sharing in their joy in my own quiet way. And this is what I tried to convey to my team. Again, to quote Terry Pettit: "These unspoken truths are / What we take with us."[65] For me, the unspoken truth is that our victory would have been another win in a good season, but the other team's victory created a joyful, memorable moment.

Did you ever experience a time when the other team won and you shared in their joy? Can you even imagine getting to that place? If not, consider this: The other team could not have had that victory were it not for your team's presence and for all the inspiration both teams put into the effort. *That* is true competition!

BOX SCORE: How competitive are you in the true sense of the word? Does your game or sideline behavior reflect a respect for the other team or individual?

Bring to mind a fierce rivalry. See them enter your field, stadium, arena, or court. See all the players without judgment. Go up to each player. Look in their eyes. Thank them for coming to compete with you—to seek together *with* you.

Play the game in your mind. Can you keep your competitive energy and let it fuel you instead of fueling the other team? Does your need to win override your joy in the game? What is your understanding of the idea of "win-win"? How can you be a true fan of the game? *Can* you be a true fan of the game? Just once, can you get dressed in the morning and put on your biggest rival's team colors?

# Community
## "to have charge of together"
## (to become one, again)

**Community (kuh-myoo-ni-tee)**

*noun:*

a body of people living in the same place under the same laws; society at large[66]

*If you were all alone in the universe with no one to talk to, no one with which to share the beauty of the stars, to laugh with, to touch, what would be your purpose in life? It is other life, it is love, which gives your life meaning. This is harmony. We must discover the joy of each other, the joy of challenge, the joy of growth.*

—Mitsugi Saotome

*One great, strong, unselfish soul in every community could actually redeem the world.*

—Elbert Hubbard

*In our hectic, fast-paced, consumer-driven society, it's common to feel overwhelmed, isolated, and alone. Many are re-discovering the healing and empowering role that community can bring to our lives. The sense of belonging we feel when we make the time to take an active role in our communities can give us a deeper sense of meaning and purpose.*

—Robert Alan

Baseball's spring training is an impressive example of community. Annually, people make the pilgrimage to spring training as if to Mecca. People crave that new energy: the rebirth, the Easter of baseball, the beginning of any season. If you have never experienced spring training, it is a part of baseball that makes for a great road trip. Just go and be around the new kids, the wise old-timers, and the All-Stars who earn the fat paychecks—all in the same place, playing a game known as the national pastime. For a few weeks each spring, the "club" is one, all levels train together, and the feeling and sense of renewal, possibility, and community is overwhelming.

Because both of our sons were attending spring training with the Detroit Tigers in Lakeland, Florida, Jim and I, as parents, joined in on the new season during a week in mid-March. The "Old English 'D'" appeared everywhere from tee shirts and shorts to flip-flops, hotel doors, and motor bikes. It's the identification with the parent club, the marking of community that made everyone feel at home, no matter where they hailed from: California, Texas, Michigan, Iowa, Venezuela, or the Dominican Republic. Players, fans, staff—we were all one.

# Redefining the Word

The word *community* comes from a combination of the Latin prefix *com*, which means "together" and either the Etruscan word *munis,* which means "to have charge of" or *munere,* which means "to give among each other." *To have charge of together.* Just like competition, when considered in this way, community demands a sense of ownership whether at spring training or in a world cup soccer stadium or in the bleachers at your local YMCA. Having been a part of the "volleyball community" for thirty-five years, I find it is rather like a family. There are caretakers, strange uncles, historians, fun cousins, people who are like your siblings, and people whom you would rather avoid. But we're bonded, brought together, by the call of this sport. There are seasonal rituals, births and deaths, successes and failures. There is accepted attire that seems to evolve over time. People tend to know and define you as a member of this community. Which community attracts you? Football, soccer, running, basketball, swimming, cheerleading, gymnastics, golf, baseball, softball—name your community and celebrate it!

# Global Community

This gathering, this united sense of purpose in support of oneness reminds us of our ultimate interconnectedness as humans sharing one planet. Ultimately, the spiritual journey takes us here, and sport can be a vehicle, as Wayne Teasdale writes in *The Mystic Heart*: "In ordinary life, of course, this feeling of solidarity comes in fleeting moments—at sports events, parties, family reunions, even political demonstrations—in those rare times of extremity when people come together." But, he goes on to point out: "The point is to apply this knowledge all the time. As we walk the mystical path, we become more and more aware of our mystical connection with everyone and everything else. And the spiritual life requires that we are ready to respond to the suffering of those we meet along the way because they are connected to us."[67]

The Olympic Games are an impressive community too, events through which people of the world, acting in accord with global ideals, come together through sport, playing games overseen by an impartial international contingent. The Olympics are growing in magnitude, visibility, and economic impact with each quadrennial. But no matter how big the Olympics themselves grow, the inspiration remains. You see it in the Olympians' faces during opening ceremonies, in their competition, and in their cooperation. Olympic Villages house thousands of athletes from every corner of the world in what is the epitome of international understanding, beyond the boundaries of political division.

The Olympic community is a human manifestation of a lesson that Earth has known and has been teaching humankind for eons. In ancient times, our ancestors may have understood this lesson better than modern humans, especially in economically developed countries, do today. This lesson is summarized beautifully in the writings of Donella Meadows, who was an adjunct professor at Dartmouth College and director of the Sustainability Institute in Hartland, Vermont, prior to her death in 2001. In her essay "The Laws of the Earth and the Laws of Economics," Meadows succinctly illustrates the relationship between community and competition.

> The first commandment of economics is: Grow. Grow forever. Companies must get bigger. National economies need to swell by a certain percent each year. People should want more, make more, earn more, spend more, ever more.

> The first commandment of the Earth is: Enough. Just so much and no more. Just so much soil. Just so much water. Just so much sunshine.

> Everything born of the Earth grows to its appropriate size and then stops. The planet does not get bigger, it gets better. Its creatures learn, mature, diversify, evolve, create amazing beauty and novelty and complexity, but live within absolute limits.

> Now, when there's an inconsistency between human economics and the laws of planet Earth, which do you think is going to win?

> Economics says: Compete. Only by pitting yourself against a worthy opponent will you perform efficiently. The reward for successful competition will be growth. You will eat up your opponents, one by one, and as you do, you will gain the resources to do it some more.

The Earth says: Compete, yes, but keep your competition in bounds. Don't annihilate. Take only what you need. Leave your competitor enough to live. Wherever possible, don't compete, cooperate. Pollinate each other, create shelter for each other, build firm structures that lift smaller species up to the light. Pass around the nutrients, share the territory. Some kinds of excellence rise out of competition; other kinds rise out of cooperation. You're not in a war, you're in a community.[68]

## Community and Coherence

The Joy Conference I attended in Indianapolis in 2002, where I first heard about sport being a spiritual pursuit, was a transformative event that has found its way into my daily life. Among the presenters were representatives from HeartMath, a California-based research and development company founded in 1991 to explore the connection between the heart, the brain, and emotions. Almost twenty years later, research and articles affirm the heart/brain/emotion link so much so that the Institute is now working toward what they have termed "global coherence."

Coherence is another word with Latin origins with a meaning similar to that of community. That is, while community means to "*come* together," coherence means to "*stick* together" in work and in play, in hard times and in good.

At the conference, HeartMath researchers presented the concept that coherence is that state in which the heart, mind, emotions, and other systems of the body function in a concert of synchronization with one another. This synchronization affords clarity of thought and action, calmness, nurturing relationships, care, purity, increased health, well-being, and purpose.

For some people, interaction with others can be a stimulus for stress. But in community, we also have more support—more fans—to help us deal with stress. This balance of stress creation and stress relief is even more pronounced within sport where the force of opposition is as intense as the power of connection. If we heed how our bodies respond to external stimuli, we feel that stress hits us in the gut while support touches our heart. Both impact the mind, either as worry or relief.

This is why, in addition to working toward individual and group wellness and world peace, HeartMath has inspired several projects within sport. I've included three examples involving golf, baseball, and volleyball.

## GOLF

Jaime Diaz is an American sports writer who specializes in golf, one of the most obvious heart/brain/emotion sports known to man, as evidenced by stories of golfers breaking clubs or throwing golf balls in disgust with their individual performance. His article, which appeared in *Golf Digest* magazine in May 2007, featured HeartMath and its emWave Personal Stress Reliever' as a top innovation that's changing the game of golf. The article explains HeartMath's research on the physiology of emotion and performance; it includes interviews with top golf coaches about the benefits of utilizing HeartMath's tools and techniques on, and off, the course.[69]

Similarly, a health-and-fitness article by author, speaker, and performance consultant David Breslow on the Golf Channel website in June 2008 states, "The truth is, the mind and heart are connected. Although science separates them as being different organs, they are not separate in terms of how each of us produces outcomes on the golf course or in life." The article reports that "emotion triggers a more powerful flow of energy in the body than the intellect." And, "The heart, which is connected to attributes such as desire, passion, energy, emotion, confidence, embracing adversity, and loving the moment...is the driving force we all have access to."[70]

## BASEBALL

In baseball, much has been spoken and written about the driving force of the Curse of the Bambino on the Boston Red Sox. In the documentary *The Joy of Sox: Weird Science and the Power of Intention,* psychiatrist Rick Leskowitz, filmmaker Joel Leskowitz, and producer Karen Webb examine the curse as well as science and spirituality on the Red Sox and their fans, known as The Red Sox Nation. The documentary's purpose, according to the article, is to "explore the power of prayer and the question of whether the good wishes of 30,000 fans might actually impact the fortunes of the home team."

Probing into this question, Rick Leskowitz submitted himself to a test by HeartMath. He was blindfolded and had earplugs placed in his ears. Sitting near him, a group of people focused on regulating their heart rhythms. "As they did so," the article reports, "Leskowitz's heart rate also became regular, he said, which is supposed to help bring forth positive emotions. In other words, the experiment suggested that emotional energy is contagious." The article quotes Leskowitz as saying, "Our theory is that the fans get into this state of high appreciation and create some kind of energy field that impacts the players."[71]

## VOLLEYBALL

As I explored this phenomenon of emotion as a contagion, which is certainly evident during post-season play as well as among rioting mobs, I learned more about how close interaction with others—those sitting side by side in the bleachers or pushing against one another to burn an effigy—increases the power of emotion. Through technological devices designed to measure the biological effect of emotions, HeartMath people can actually measure a person's coherent energy via the heart rate rhythm as much as six feet away. In addition, they can measure coherence, or lack of it, in someone else's brainwaves who is in close proximity to that person. In other words, if I were six feet or less away from you and technicians attached an electroencephalography (EEG) to *my* head, they could read *your* level of coherence.

The significance of this measurement of six feet confirmed something I had always intuitively known about volleyball, a game in which six people play in a thirty-foot by thirty-foot area. All within six feet of each other, volleyball players *all* affect each other! This confirmation told me that, as a coach, I needed to help my players get to that place of coherence where we would become a *team* in the greatest sense of the word—sticking together to experience success.

I saw the impact of this connectivity recently when I inserted a freshman who had never played before into a match. The first time, I inserted her when the five around her were able to help her get to a good emotional place on the court. But in the next instance, she had to go in at an inopportune moment due to a disciplinary situation with another player. I could feel her fear. So could the other players on our team, those on the court and those off. The team leaders said the energy was different the second time, and during a time-out, there seemed to be a cartoon bubble above the freshman's head that read: "Is it me? Is it me?" No, it was the coherent energy of all.

Our team leaders, fortunately, have come to the point where they are also aware of this coherent energy. They recognize it, believe in its positive power, and want to experience more of it on the court and in their lives. They are telling me, "We have to get to this place." My role as a coach is to help them get there and to recognize, with them, when they are. I say to the team leaders, "You are in coherence. Help the others on the court get there too."

In contrast to the semi-cozy aspects of volleyball, I couldn't help but think about athletes who compete in solo sports, like golf or horseracing or long-distance running. Or even baseball, a sport in which the pitcher, the key defensive player on the team, performs in a virtual vacuum on the mound, separated from all other teammates by a distance greater than six feet. These athletes epitomize Yogi Berra's oxymoron, "Baseball is 90 percent mental; the other half is physical."[72] Let's take a mental time-out here to reconsider our game.

TIME-OUT: go to www.heartmath.org and look around the site to learn more about the science of HeartMath.

Consider a sport you play or follow. Are you a wrestler who is in direct physical contact with another and therefore either affecting or being effected? Or are you a football player, who sets up in great proximity at the line of scrimmage? Or are you a lone competitor in games such as in golf, tennis, figure skating, or diving? Can you see how coherence or lack of it affects your performance?

## Coherence Technique

To gain coherence, HeartMath teaches us to breathe three intentional breaths to silence and empty the mind. It suggests that we "let go" and, in a spiritual way of functioning in the world, "let God." When we try too hard to make things happen, we become disentrained, incoherent, and ineffective. But when we let go and trust in our knowing and our innate—some would say God-given—ability, the process unfolds like a hot knife cutting effortlessly through butter.

As a coach, I find this is the hardest idea to teach. But I believe there is something to this process and that Phil Jackson is on to something when he teaches his NBA superstars to meditate prior to games.[73] From Jackson's relationships with Michael Jordan and the Chicago Bulls to Kobe Bryant and the Los Angeles Lakers, his pregame ritual of silence, meditation, and/or contemplation continues.

HeartMath confirms to the volleyball community that ours is a peaceful sport by virtue of the rules: there is no physical contact with the other team; teams are separated by the illusion of a net; and only physical skill, mental acuity, and team coherence determines success.

Too often, sport coaches and staff focus on the other team with scouting. They rely on film and other technologies that amount to legitimized spying to find flaws and weaknesses in the other team when, in fact, the focus should be on improving our individual and team strengths. Legendary basketball coach John Wooden emphasized this when he wrote, "I seldom mentioned the other team. I believe it takes away from the concentration on ourselves in the preparation."[74] His bestseller, *Wooden: A Lifetime of Observations and Reflections On and Off the Court*, simply instructs coaches and players in ways of victory. His section on scouting concludes:

> Perhaps we gained an advantage by having so much confidence in our own ability to play near our potential (because of our detailed and disciplined preparation) that it kept us from becoming fearful of another team.

> It goes back to focusing on what you can control. We had no control over the many possible variations an opponent might use in a game. We did have control, total control, over preparing to execute our game. To me, it made more sense to concentrate on that.[75]

From the heart of a master teacher and coach comes affirmation of an age-old simple wisdom: Know thyself.

## Heart Community

HeartMath demands that we ask the deeper question: What is in your heart? This affirms Joseph Chilton Pearce's writing about the physiology and origination of the heart. Pearce said that the heart precedes the brain in embryonic development and that there are neurons and brain cells located within the heart.[76] Engaging with the heart first allows us to access the One, the oneness, the connection, the *re-ligio* (linking back) to our source, the one source of all. This is our very first, primal awareness that comes to us from deep within the womb. And as we reflect on sportuality, it does not matter what sport we involve ourselves in, there is always a community within that sport: those who have charge of it together.

Teams are communities. Each sport is a community. Sport in general is a community. All are members of the global community. And every now and then, opportunities arise to transform the global community through sport, and it is the coherent soul who takes advantage of the inspiration it can provide. Examples of healing communities include John Fetzer and the 1968 Detroit Tigers, Nelson Mandela with both the 1995 Rugby World Cup and the 2010 Soccer World Cup, and the 2009-10 New Orleans Saints.

## *1968 Detroit Tigers*

The 1968 baseball season occurred in a year of upheaval. The Tet Offensive earlier in the year increased opposition to the Vietnam War. The city of Detroit had suffered through one of the worst race riots in American history during the summer of 1967. Less than a week before Opening Day, Martin Luther King, Jr. was assassinated in Memphis, triggering civil unrest in sixty American cities. The assassination of Robert Kennedy followed in June. Interestingly, that same weekend, the Detroit Tigers played and split a series against the White Sox in Chicago. And in late August, Chicago police had violent confrontations with thousands of anti-war protesters during the tumultuous Democratic National Convention.

Yet, through the summer of 1968, the people of Detroit were united by their passion for the Tigers and the calming radio voice of legendary Hall of Fame broadcaster, Ernie Harwell. When the Tigers won the World Series, the headline in the *Detroit Free Press* read: "WE WIN!" The headline told the story. Amidst all the turmoil, the people of Detroit came together behind their baseball team—and the people and the community of Detroit were winners.

In a column published on October 11, 1968, *Detroit Free Press* senior baseball writer, Joe Falls, described the impact of the Tigers championship on the city:

My town, as you know, had the worst riot in our nation's history in the summer of 1967, and it left scars which may never fully heal. . . . And so, as 1968 dawned and we all started thinking ahead to the hot summer nights in Detroit, the mood of our city was taut. It was apprehensive. . . . But then something started happening in the middle of 1968. You could pull up to a light at the corner of Clairmount and 12th, which was the hub of last year's riot, and the guy in the next car would have his radio turned up: 'McLain looks in for the sign, he's set. Here's the pitch.' . . . It was a year when an entire community, an entire city, was caught up in a wild, wonderful frenzy.[77]

Even the Governor of Michigan, George Romney, credited the Tigers with helping calm the city. In a letter to Tigers owner, John Fetzer, Romney wrote:

The deepest meaning of this victory extends beyond the sports pages, radio broadcasts, and the telecasts that have consumed our attention for several months. This championship occurred when all of us in Detroit and Michigan needed a great lift. At a time of unusual tensions, when many good men lost their perspective toward others, the Tigers set an example of what human relations should really be.[78]

These were *my* Tigers too. I had just turned ten years old, and my teacher at Smith Elementary in Plymouth, Michigan, brought a TV into my fifth-grade classroom at a time when that was simply unheard of. While the city of Detroit celebrated joy in its community, twenty-four fifth graders in Mr. Somerville's class felt it as well.

## 1995 RUGBY WORLD CUP

The movie *Invictus,* which was nominated for an Oscar in 2009, tells the inspiring true story of how Nelson Mandela enlisted the captain of South Africa's rugby team to help unite their country. In 1994, newly elected President Mandela knew his nation was racially and economically divided in the wake of apartheid. Believing he could bring his people together through the universal language of sport, Mandela rallied South Africa's team, an underdog, as they made their historic run to the 1995 Rugby World Cup Championship. Their championship proved, as he said, "Sport has the power to change the world. It has the power to unite people in a way that little else does. Sport can awaken hope where there was previously only despair."[79]

While the movie, starring Morgan Freeman and Matt Damon, is based on fact, producer Clint Eastwood did take one creative liberty that is worth noting here. The movie's title comes from the fact that Mandela, the 1993 Nobel Peace Prize recipient, incarcerated for twenty-seven years in prison in Robben Island near Cape Town, survived through the powerful words of the poem "Invictus" by William Ernest Henly. In the movie, Mandela gives the poem to his national rugby team's captain, Francois Pienaar. In reality, Mandela provided Pienaar with an extract from "The Man in the Arena," a speech delivered by U.S. President Theodore Roosevelt in 1910:

> It is not the critic who counts; not the man who points out how the strong man stumbles, or where the doer of deeds could have done them better. The credit belongs to the man who is actually in the arena, whose face is marred by dust and sweat and blood; who strives valiantly; who errs, who comes short again and again, because there is no effort without error and shortcoming; but who does actually strive to do the deeds; who knows great enthusiasms, the great devotions; who spends himself in a worthy cause; who at the best knows in the end the triumph of high achievement, and who at the worst, if he fails, at least fails while daring greatly, so that his place shall never be with those cold and timid souls who neither know victory nor defeat.[80]

Compare Roosevelt's speech, "The Man in the Arena," to Henley's "Invictus":

*Out of the night that covers me,*
*Black as the Pit from pole to pole,*
*I thank whatever gods may be*
*For my unconquerable soul.*
*In the fell clutch of circumstance*
*I have not winced nor cried aloud.*
*Under the bludgeonings of chance*
*My head is bloody, but unbowed.*
*Beyond this place of wrath and tears*
*Looms but the Horror of the shade,*
*And yet the menace of the years*
*Finds, and shall find, me unafraid.*
*It matters not how strait the gate,*
*How charged with punishments the scroll,*
*I am the master of my fate:*
*I am the captain of my soul.*[81]

Is one of these more sportual than the other? I think not. Both to me have a sportual focus. Both invoke the true competitor strength, spirit, perseverance, and attitude. Both, together, are far more challenging than either one, or the other alone.

## *2010 MEN'S WORLD CUP SOCCER*

World Cup Soccer, or as the rest of the world says "Football" or "Futbol," grabs our attention every four years. (2010 was the men's world cup; women play each four years the year after the men.) The 2010 tournament was particularly engaging for the United States because media has made it increasingly accessible to everyone and the U.S. team was involved, making it to the round of sixteen teams before losing to Uruguay. Eventually, Spain defeated the Netherlands in the final but not before the entire world community was aware that again something special was happening in South Africa, the tournament's 2010 host. You need only to go to the website of soccer's governing body, the Federation Internationale de Football Association (FIFA), to see sportual messages about the games and an open letter from FIFA's president Joseph Blatter, which ends with the following:

This World Cup had a special momentum, linked with a history of freedom and the living history of one man. This man is still living, at the age of 92, and this is a man who has suffered so much. But despite this, upon his release from prison, he spoke of peace and understanding. I met him for the first time in 1992 and he had a dream—to bring the World Cup to his country. The dream came true in May 2004 when South Africans were awarded the 2010 FIFA World Cup. He brought the World Cup to South Africa. He wanted to attend the tournament—and last night he fulfilled that ambition. So I must pay homage to the greatest living humanist—Nelson 'Mandiba' Mandela.[82]

## Super Bowl *XLIV*

Lastly, Super Bowl XLIV in South Florida featured the Indianapolis Colts and the New Orleans Saints in the winter of 2010. In the stuff that movies are made of, the Saints bucked the odds and won 31-17, living a Cinderella story and igniting the soul of that city on the Gulf of Mexico coast still physically, economically, and spiritually affected by Hurricane Katrina. The entire country seemed to be rooting for the Saints, athletic representatives of a hurting community; as a nation, we saw the game and the victory as a means for continued healing.

# The Community of Football

Here in the United States, when discussing football, we often use terms of domination and violence. However, anthropologist Conrad Kottak has a different idea. As a professor of Anthropology at the University of Michigan since 1968, much of his work is based on Madagascar and South America, but the content of his latest textbook, *Cultural Anthropology*, talks about football and its relationship to American culture, religious congregations, and business work teams.

By popular definitions, congregation applies to people who assemble for religious worship. Kottak applies a broader definition, including people who gather to watch a game, either among student-athletes or professionals. Thus, congregation is not a community only within a church but also a community in the arena of sport. And because religions, for the most part, preach peace and fellowship, Kottak reminds us that we can apply those precepts to the sport community as well.

> Football, we say, is only a game, yet it has become a hugely popular spectator sport. On fall Saturdays, millions of people travel to and from college football games. Smaller congregations meet in high school stadiums. Millions of Americans watch televised football. Indeed, nearly half the adult population of the United States watches the Super Bowl, which attracts fans of diverse ages, ethnic backgrounds, regions, religions, political parties, jobs, social statuses, levels of wealth, and genders.

Kottak also quotes the work of anthropologists Susan Montague and Robert Morais (1981) who, he says, "argue that Americans appreciate football because it presents a miniaturized and simplified version of modern organizations."

> Montague and Morais link football's values, particularly teamwork, to those associated with business. Like corporate workers, the ideal players are diligent and dedicated to the team. Within corporations, however, decision making is complicated, and workers aren't always rewarded for their dedication and good job performance. Decisions are simpler and rewards are more consistent in football, these anthropologists contend, and this helps explain its popularity. Even if we can't figure out how Exxon-Mobil or Microsoft run, any fan can become an expert on football's rules, teams, scores, statistics, and patterns of play. Even more important, football suggests that the values stressed by business really do pay off. Teams whose members work the hardest, show the most spirit,

and best develop and coordinate their talents can be expected to win more often than other teams do.[83]

# Believing in Community

Throughout the volleyball season of 2002, my team slowly woke to the possibilities of what they could do together. I'd like to think it's the fact that I promised to get a tattoo if they won the conference tournament, but truthfully, with our youth, inexperience, and injury rate that year, I felt confident that I'd avoid the tattoo parlor for one more year. We had finished third in the regular season, which matched us up with the second-place team for the tournament semi-finals. While we had lost twice to this team already, my two seniors apparently were not ready to finish.

For the first two-and-a-half games of the five-game match, it was business as usual: we had lost the first two games and were losing the third. But something happened at the midpoint of game three that brought us out of the depths: we had a critical mass of believers who refused to stop playing. Now, I believe that success and winning is a choice, and I saw it on that crisp, fall day in Alma, Michigan.

My assistant coach and I had to hold each other down to prevent ourselves from any sort of coaching (or over-coaching) or calling time-outs because our team was playing with a belief, a spirit unlike anything I had ever experienced. We were wise enough to know that our coaching was over for this match. Our words could no longer serve those players because they had found at this eleventh hour what we and they had been working toward since the first preseason practice.

They were coherent and focused. They no longer saw the team on the other side of the net as an opponent but as a source of energy to fuel them. They, literally, had reached that lofty level of really competing. And they chose to win.

That was one moment of community that will stay with me forever, and it is the thing that upsets are made of: reaching the state of community, a group of believers.

*Believe.* Baseball's Tug McGraw said it: "You gotta believe!" Believe in yourself and your teammates. You are *one*. We seek unity together.

We have charge of this together. These are the messages that team heard on a daily basis throughout the season, and the ones they chose to live out as they played toward the championship. They believed so strongly that instead of time-outs being filled with volleyball-related strategies, all I heard was the chant, "tattoo . . . tattoo . . . tattoo." I knew that this community was focused on one thing and that they wouldn't stop until they got there . . . and got me there . . . to the tattoo parlor, where I permanently inked the Chinese character for "believe" on my right shoulder blade.

BOX SCORE:

Why are you drawn to people who have "heart"? How does your life reflect what is in your heart for yourself and for others? Can you see how what is in your heart manifests in your community, your team, your family? Do you realize that your emotions affect your performance? How do you manage or access those emotions?

Consider the communities where you belong. What areas of your life are "community" where you experience coherence together with others? Does this describe your family? Your workplace? Your team? Your city . . . state . . . country . . . planet?

# THIRD QUARTER:
## Enthusiasm, Humor, Education

# Enthusiasm
## "to know God within"
## (self-realization)

**Enthusiasm (en-thu-ze'-a-zem)**

*noun:*

strong warmth of feeling, keen interest, fervor; absorbing or controlling possession of the mind by any interest or pursuit, lively interest; an occupation, activity, or pursuit in which such interest is shown; extreme religious devotion, usually associated with intense emotionalism and a break with orthodoxy.[84]

*Nothing great was ever achieved without enthusiasm.*
> —Ralph Waldo Emerson

*Enthusiasm moves the world.*
> —Arthur James Balfour

*Enthusiasm is contagious. Be a carrier.*
> —Susan Rabin

*It's faith in something and enthusiasm for something that makes life worth living.*

—Oliver Wendell Holmes


*None are so old as those who have outlived enthusiasm.*

—Henry David Thoreau


While all of these great philosophers and writers obviously praise the value of enthusiasm, playwright Tennessee Williams has gone so far as to make the ultimate statement of praise: "Enthusiasm is the most important thing in life."

My volleyball coach at the University of Michigan was a native of Shanghai, so his words reflected a Chinese flavor. He always called me "en-susiastic," which I grew to accept *who* I was and *what* I brought to the game. It wouldn't be until years later when I ran across an origin of the word that I began to appreciate it at a much deeper, more meaningful, and, yes, a sportual level.

## Redefining the Word

The word *enthusiasm* comes from the Late Latin *enthusiasmus* as well as the Greek *enthousiasmos*, both of which mean "possession by a god," or "having a god within." Looking closer at the opening syllables, we see this literal connection with God. *En* is the Latin and Greek word for "in" or "within," and *theo* in Latin and *theos* in Greek are the words for "god" in those languages.

*Theo* is often used in the formation of compound words, such as theocracy, a form of government in which god or a deity is recognized as the supreme civil ruler; theocrat, a person who rules or governs as a representative of god or a deity; theosophy, a form of philosophical or religious thought based on a mystical insight into the divine nature.

# Enthusiasm Within

God within! Enthusiasm is an outward sign of God-within! The joy shows!

In the follow-up to his bestseller *A New Earth,* author and spiritual teacher Eckhart Tolle writes in *Oneness With All Life:*

> Enthusiasm means there is a deep enjoyment in what you do plus the added element of a goal or vision that you work toward. When you add a goal to the enjoyment of what you do, the energy-field or vibrational frequency changes. . . . At the height of creative activity fueled by enthusiasm, there will be enormous intensity and energy behind what you do. You will feel like an arrow that is moving toward the target—and enjoying the journey. . . . Enthusiasm knows where it is going, but at the same time, it is deeply at one with the present moment, the source of aliveness, its joy and its power.[85]

Look within. How enthusiastic are you? Do you see your enthusiasm? Can you feel your power, your God within?

Look around you. Is your enthusiasm visible? Can your coaches, teammates, friends, parents, or children see your God within?

Teams, owners, and sport marketers always talk about filling the stands with fans. Consider, as an athlete, asking, "Why would people want to come and watch me play? What can they receive from the game?" They can receive your enthusiasm. They can receive the God within that you share. Think about it. Do you engage in games simply to feel better, if only by watching?

Now, you could say that it's easy to be enthusiastic when there are hundreds, thousands, or even millions of people watching you perform. And that's true. The hard part, or actually the sportual part, for an athlete is to convey enthusiasm when no one is watching: during practices; in team functions; indeed, in everyday life, moment by moment, by remaining present to the purpose of sport as an expression of talent.

The Bible speaks of a master who entrusted three of his servants with a certain number of talents, and then went away on business. Two of the servants used those talents and created more talents, but one servant buried his talents. When the master returned, he praised the two servants who used and created more talents, and he chastised the servant who kept his talent hidden.[86] In this parable, we can easily identify the *master* as God, but the word *talent* requires a bit more explanation. In biblical times, a *talent* was a coin that represented a certain amount of money. Today, we know talent as a skill that each person is born with, a gift from God to be utilized and honed for the greatest possible benefit for the person and those nearby. Each person (each servant, if you will) has a certain talent: to play sport, to create music or poetry, to perform well in finance or business, to listen and counsel or coach others.

Each of those talents, however large or small, is a gift from God. In fact, *those talents*—your talents—are your God within. *Those talents* are your real "ensusiasm." And, speaking as a coach, those are the talents I want in the athletes on my team.

## Shared Enthusiasm

Minor league baseball has grown tremendously in this country since 1941 when Bill Veeck began promoting baseball at that level. Veeck, as a franchise owner, was an entrepreneur and promoter from Chicago who was one of the first to make the fan experience important. His antics included several outlandish promotions designed to attract and entertain the fans, such as the appearance of Eddie Gaedel on August 19, 1951. Gaedel, the shortest player in the history of the major leagues at 3'7", made his only plate appearance in the bottom of the first wearing elf-like shoes and the number "1/8" on his uniform. He walked on four straight pitches before being replaced by a pinch runner.[87]

Today, however, perhaps because of the economics of it all, a family can attend a minor league game for a fraction of what it costs to visit a major league park. The West Michigan Whitecaps, the A-level farm team for the Detroit Tigers that both my sons played for in Grand Rapids, Michigan, drew crowds of several thousand on a regular basis. The excitement was there. The desire was there. And, indeed, so was the enthusiasm. These guys all want to make it to the big leagues, and people go to see the games because every one of us has a drive to also make it big somehow someday—to use and capitalize on our talents. People go to see these young men perform because of how it makes them *feel*.

The genius of any club owner is revealed with the level of fan support for the team. Of course, this translates into financial gain for the owner, but people also gain that joy and satisfaction of watching the team compete.

An aphorism for success in business is "see the need and fill it." I believe there is a spiritual need deep within all of us to connect, to be inspired, to find unity, to get to the One, to be whole, to be healed. Because sports can help us accomplish that, people will always come to watch—and root and cheer, even when the team is losing. *That* is sportual enthusiasm. It's like the final scene in *Field of Dreams* in which we see headlights lined up for miles just to see Ray's field. As the movie script says, they "won't know why" but they will simply come. It's shared enthusiasm for the common goal that unites us all.

## Expressing Enthusiasm

Children, of course, are innately enthusiastic. It's like they are still tapped into that spiritual awareness of God—*theos*—within them.

The Christian Scriptures read: "At that time the disciples came to Jesus, saying, 'Who is the greatest in the kingdom of heaven?' And calling to him a child, he put him in the midst of them and said, 'Truly, I say to you, unless you turn and become like children, you will never enter the kingdom of heaven.'"[88]

Bring to mind the picture of anyone of any age, whether playing baseball or softball, rounding third and heading for home after hitting a game-winning home run in the final inning. They are skipping, jumping, and smiling, even laughing, thoroughly enjoying the accomplishment of coming home. Certainly you've seen moments like those in sport. Perhaps you've been there yourself.

And the joy of such accomplishment need not be within baseball. The Christian message encourages us to "Seek first the kingdom of heaven,"[89] where the kingdom of heaven is within. In other words, sport *demands* that we live our enthusiasm, that we *show* our God within! That is why the sports photos that sell are those of victory piles, team dances, and one player nestled in the arms of another.

TIME-OUT:

Go to the Sportuality facebook page to relive some of the moments listed below and others.

Consider these great moments of enthusiasm in sport.

- Jim Valvano after winning the NCAA Men's Basketball national championship.
- Fans pouring out onto the field or court.
- Tiger Woods making the putt and celebrating with his caddy.
- Sergio Garcia dancing down the fairway.
- Victorious teams dancing around with each other like children.
- The catcher picking up and hugging the pitcher after a no-hitter.
- Champagne sprays in many sports and the victor's milk bath at the Indy 500.
- Brandi Chastain from the U.S. ripping off her shirt after scoring the game winning goal in 1999 at the Women's Soccer World Cup. (She has since written a book titled *It's Not About the Bra: How to Play Hard, Play Fair, and Put the Fun Back into Competitive Sports* by Brandi Chastain, Gloria Averbuch.)

Mascots, cheerleaders, musicians, bare-chested men with one giant letter per chest all serve as fuel for enthusiasm. Media attention, sportswriters, challenges, and rivalries all give us permission or actually demand that we show enthusiasm. Consider the similar spirit moving through a walk-off home run, a by-a-nose victory at the Kentucky Derby, a Martin Luther King, Jr. speech, a church filled with worshippers, or a Quaker Meeting. Whether uproarious or subdued, whether cheering or silently observing, God is there . . . within.

## The Memorable, Enthusiastic Bird

One of the most memorable enthusiastic athletes in my life passed away on April 13, 2009. Mark "The Bird" Fidrych came to Detroit in 1976 and took the town by storm. His enthusiasm, his love of life, his treatment of teammates and opponents alike was unlike anything anyone in Detroit, or even the country, had ever seen. The lanky, 6'3" right-handed pitcher resembled *Sesame Street*'s Big Bird, earning him the nickname of "The Bird." Fidrych captured the imagination of fans with his antics on the field. He would crouch down on the pitcher's mound and fix cleat marks in a ritual that became known as "manicuring the mound." He would talk to himself, talk to the ball, aim the ball like a dart, strut around the mound after every out, and throw back balls that "had hits in them," insisting they be removed from the game. Mark Fidrych also was known for shaking everyone's hand after a game.

Mark had a true joy for the game, and it showed in the success he enjoyed while with the Tigers, starting with the All-Star game in 1976. He won the Rookie of the Year Award and was Cy Young Award runner-up that same year.

Unfortunate knee and shoulder injuries kept him from ever replicating his rookie season, but God was there, within Mark and all those he influenced along the way. Detroit—and baseball—hasn't seen the likes of him since.[90]

BOX SCORE:

How do you approach your game? What kind of player are you? What kind of fan are you?

How do you manifest your enthusiasm? Can you be enthusiastic even when others around you don't share your enthusiasm? Can you be enthusiastic for the other team and their level of play even when they're beating your team?

What do people say about you after they watch you play? What do your teammates say about you and your level of enthusiasm? Do they see your *theos*—God in you?

Who is your enthusiastic role model? What are your favorite images of enthusiasm in any sport?

Most people are enthusiastic in some way and to some degree, but some express enthusiasm in different ways. Some outwardly demonstrate enthusiasm, and others are more subdued. How do you express yours?

# Humor
## "to be fluid and flexible like water"
## (attitude)

**Humor (hyü-mer)**

*noun:*

a comic, absurd, or incongruous quality that causes amusement; the faculty of perceiving or expressing what is amusing or comical; comical writing or talk, such as comic books, skits, and plays; mental disposition or temperament; (in Medieval philosophy) one of the four elemental fluids of the body—blood, phlegm, black bile, and yellow bile—regarded as determining, by their relative proportions, a person's physical and mental temperament; an often temporary state of mind imposed by circumstances; a sudden, unpredictable, or unreasoning inclination, such as a whim; that quality which appeals to a sense of the ludicrous or absurdly incongruous.[91]

*Laughter is a holy thing. It is as sacred as music and silence and solemnity, maybe more sacred. Laughter is like a prayer, like a bridge over which creatures tiptoe to meet each other. Laughter is like mercy; it heals. When you can laugh at yourself, you are free.*

—Ted Loder

It was the semi-final match of Division I NCAA national volleyball tournament, and one team had won the first two games of the match. The other team huddled around its coach, searching for wisdom, and the only thing this coach felt he could do was to tell his team that no matter what happened in this match he loved them. Out of the edge of a huddle came a voice proclaiming, "Coach, you're not going to get my Bud Light," a statement referring to the highly successful beer commercials of that era that attracted attention and consumers with their humor. The team who had received the dose of humor returned to the court, laughing, happy, and relaxed. Even the spectators could sense a palpable difference in the team's demeanor and energy.

Their coach had taken the risk of expressing personal emotion, making a statement that might have seemed out of place—incongruous. In return, that player took a risk and responded with comic absurdity. The team experienced humor—a change in disposition and temperament. The result was that they won the match and went on to win the national championship.

Of course, several factors were present in addition to the humor, including talent, resolve, and great coaching, but the humorous moment opened everyone up to a shared purpose. That incident, which I witnessed as a fan, but have also read about since, still makes me smile.

## Redefining the Word

Considering that today the word *humor* evokes images of comedy or intense bouts of laughter, it is interesting that its roots come from Middle English (*humour*), Anglo-French (*umor, umour*), Medieval Latin (*humor*), Latin (*humēre*), Norse (*vokr*), and Greek (*hygros*) words that mean "moisture, moist, damp, and wet."[92]

Humor: To be fluid, like water. I love this way of considering humor. When we are fluid, we are flexible. We go with the flow, easily maneuvering over and around obstacles. We are like passengers in a boat with no oars, a raft floating down a river. We see a rock ahead. What do we do? We can be frightened into frenzy. Or we can see the absurdity of the situation and laugh.

Which will serve us better? I have found that humor allows us to flow around the obstacles in our lives without incident, without issue, without having to re-encounter those obstacles again and again and again. Humor is our ability to step out, take a risk, and let go of the oars. Humor is our unique ability to understand that all things are happening as they should. Humor is our ability to remain a light in the midst of darkness.

## Humor as Energy

As coaches, we try to keep our teams loose, flexible, and focused. We try to find the balance between seriousness and lightness. Why? Because we know that our players want to have fun. After all, without fun, life isn't enjoyable.

In *The Mystic Heart*, Wayne Teasdale writes about humor as a necessary part of being human:

> In my opinion, the sense of humor is the seventh "sense." We have the usual five senses, and then many see a psychic or sixth sense, but there is a sense of humor. Life is incomplete without it.
>
> A sense of humor not only expresses our natural and supernatural happiness, our contentment, it is also a very useful check against self deception. It is very easy to take ourselves much too seriously. Humor allows us to transcend our seriousness and become lighter, more inwardly free. Humor, like self knowledge, is filled with truth. It is essential for our human and spiritual evolvement.[93]

Exactly.

In recent seasons, my team has measured success by how they feel when they are playing. They have found that we can be intensely competitive but retain our humor. When humor is defined as a movement of energy, we do play with a greater freedom and flow. This may be a paradigm shift for some who believe that, if you are laughing or smiling, you cannot be focused. Indeed, laughing or smiling while focused is the state of "both/and" that we must achieve in order to really find the joy in the game and to share it with others.

My alma mater, the University of Michigan, has recently announced the "Humor at Michigan" project in which researchers will study the effects of laughter and humor on the human psyche. Dr. Daniel Herwitz, director of the Institute of the Humanities at the university, believes those who scoff at humor studies ignore humor's profound value to the academy. "I see humor as essential to the practice of keeping the university humane, if you will, and keeping it in touch with reality," he says. "The university loves to study pain and depression and sadness and suicide and all kinds of things that are upsetting. But it has relatively little to say about happiness, joy, ecstasy—the high register of life. So exploring these phenomena is not a bad thing."[94] If Dr. Herwitz is right, then there is value in the study of humor in sport as we attempt to keep *sport* humane. That's not a bad thing either.

## Sport's Humorous Characters

All sports have their "characters," those humorous personalities who are able to see themselves and their efforts with a sense of flexibility and fluidity. Yogi Berra, Harry Caray, Satchel Paige, Roger McDowell, Bob Uecker, Meadowlark Lemon and the Harlem Globetrotters, Chi Chi Rodriguez, Lee Trevino, and Dick Vitale all fit the bill.

If you are in sport, you know about these renowned international characters, and you know the stories about them—often embellished. Maybe you know someone equally funny on your team or in the sports you play and watch. You know they are always entertaining and sure to elicit a laugh or enhance a party.

I had the opportunity to meet boxing promoter Don King at Mickey Mantle's Restaurant in New York in the summer of 1998. He was with his entourage, and they were doing a radio spot to promote a fight the following weekend at Madison Square Garden. My sons approached him and asked if they could have their photo taken with him. After complying with their request, this large man with his notorious, wild Afro pulled me onto his lap as if to say, "Come and sit here, hon," and said to my husband, Jim, "*You* take *my* picture!" With his trademark cigar hanging off his lip, he quipped, "Only in America, folks. Only in America!"

# Laughter Heals

Laughter has been increasingly researched as a healing tool. Not only are we healed, we become happier with a laugh. We are wired to laugh. We laugh for lots of reasons: anger, frustration, fear, nervousness, boredom, and joy. Following are some of the benefits of laughter, discovered and studied through research, which can help us improve social interaction and create bonds between individuals and groups:

- Laughter provides enjoyable exercise.

- Laughter is a bit like an internal organ massage that leaves them invigorated and alert (Other ways are hiccupping, coughing, sobbing, and vomiting—so given a choice, I prefer laughter).

- Laughter provides isometric abdominal exercise to tone abdominal muscles.

- Laughter helps us stay healthy and even helps us manage pain or illness.

- Laughter helps protect us from colds and viruses because it increases the levels of antibodies (Immunoglobulin A) in the nose and respiratory passages.

- Laughter increases levels of natural killer (NK) cells and antibodies to boost the immune system.

- Laughter stimulates production of lymphocytes containing T-cells that deal with cancer cells.

- Laughter helps us manage pain.

- Laughter reduces blood pressure and heart rate if practiced regularly.

- Laughter engages every major system of the body.

- Laughter helps us to feel good and look good (although not always at the time!)

- Laughter is one of the best muscle relaxants.

- Laughter oxygenates our blood and increases our "feel good" factor.

- Laughter reduces stress hormones epinephrine and cortisol.

- Laughter provides facial exercise and increases blood flow to the skin.

- Laughter activates our tear glands to brighten our eyes.[95]

The athletic training room at Kalamazoo College is a great example of humor and healing. Head trainer, Scott Michel, is effective not only because of his knowledge of his craft but because of how he weaves his superior sense of humor throughout his work. The model skeleton in the corner of the training room wears the fuzzy red-and-blue top hat (or "birthday hat" to training room regulars), sunglasses, and flowered boxer shorts. Healing methods include laughter in addition to seasoned and experienced medical care. And sometimes I wonder if athletes try to find an excuse to need treatment just to be in that fun and healing environment.

# Laughter Intervention

We can promote health and well-being through humor intervention, and the greater the stage, the greater the effect on a greater number of people. Consider, for example, video share sites, such as YouTube, through which the world has access to any fun video, several of which originate in sport. Consider the popularity of "Sports Bloopers"—those unexpected, ridiculous, happy moments in which something hilarious happens and laughter is a natural reaction. But while laughter is a natural reaction toward humor, in order for it to be real, we have to laugh *at* ourselves and *with* others.

Spiritually, I have to believe Jesus practiced laughter intervention. I believe that Jesus was a fun guy who attracted people, who kept people's attention, who could tell a good story, and who knew when to be serious and when to lighten up. One of my favorite artistic renderings of Jesus is the painting of the "Laughing Jesus" by Ralph Kozak. For years, it hung in the vestibule of my church, a perfect reminder to me of the joy available in every moment. The challenge to all of us is to make the choice for joy.

We can also learn from and be inspired by the Laughing Buddha, who is not the same as Gautama Buddha, the main Buddha associated with founding Buddhism. Rather, the Laughing Buddha (also known as *Hotei* in Japan or *Pu-Tai* in China) is thought to be based on a wandering Chinese monk who lived at the time of the Liang Dynasty (907-923 AD). He is incorporated in Buddhist, Taoist, and Shinto traditions and is most often depicted with a large round tummy, laughing or smiling.

The Laughing Buddha symbolizes good luck, contentment, and abundance. The idea that you can rub the Buddha's belly to bring luck and wealth is somewhat of a recent addition and is not part of Buddhist tradition. Rubbing his belly or not, having this symbol around helps remind us that a prosperous, loving, giving life is possible on Earth.

While traveling in China with my volleyball team, shopping in a massive marketplace in Shanghai, our translator and former Chinese volleyball national team member Chris Chen helped me purchase, at a very good price, a wooden carving of Laughing Buddha. This, however, was no ordinary Laughing Buddha. He is, as the team calls him, Setting Buddha. His hands are raised above his head in a setting position, a common skill in volleyball.

This figure, all four inches of him, makes me smile with humorous memories. Not only did Chris and I share a happy moment, negotiating my cost down to one-tenth of the asking price, but the Laughing Buddha symbolizes the joy of our entire journey to China. I had gone with my team to that great nation in the Orient to reignite my joy in the game I love. The bonus was finding this little carved wooden character—setting, smiling, and reminding me on a daily basis of the infinite abundance of humor all around me—in China, in Kalamazoo—everywhere.

TIME-OUT:

Go to the Sportuality facebook page and check out the video where as the voice of Harry Caray, comedian Dan St. Paul calls the "First Baseball Game Ever Played," sometimes referred to as the "Heaven and Hell Baseball Game," and some humorous rain-delay antics from enthusiastic baseball players.:

# Baseball: A Playground of Laughter

In no sport is humor more abundant than baseball: in the bullpen, in the dugout, in the stands, during rain delays, in the broadcast booth, or in the clubhouse. Because of the nature of baseball and its long, drawn-out leisurely pace, humor is often used as a tool to stay connected, to pass time, and to keep spirits up. Plus it's *fun*! It makes you *feel* good. And stories of pranks abound. One of Andrew's favorites was inserting eighteen pine-scented car fresheners in a teammate's bag before a nine-hour bus ride to a weekend series and laughing along with the poor guy as he smelled like pine all weekend. Pranks create a light mood, but they also serve to create a deeper team connection, where one prank will usually set off a series of events that will last months, in a spirit of fun and good-heartedness.

# Timing Is Everything

Humor is about timing, as is sport. I first learned about the spirituality of baseball from humorist Steve Bhaerman, aka Swami Beyondananda. When comparing humor to pitching, Steve said, "It's all rhythm and timing, where the pitcher rules the rhythm game."[96]

It makes sense to me that Andrew is a pitcher because he has been blessed with a profoundly funny sense of humor and, when growing up, he was a drummer in a band. He has that whole rhythm and humor thing down! Even the word "pitch" has many meanings in addition to throwing a baseball: to tell a story or a joke, the tilt of a soccer field, the angle of Earth on its axis, and even black tar.

# Laughable Mascots

Mascots are yet another tool at humor, at connection, at association with fun and sport. Some of my favorites are Lil' Red from Nebraska, the Stanford Dancing Tree, and, of course, the San Diego Chicken.

### Nebraska's Lil' Red

Lil' Red is very tall with a happy, round face. With smiling eyes and mouth and a cap turned sideways on his head, he portrays the innocence of a little kid. He's part human and part helium balloon. When he walks, his upper body sways from side to side, and he looks like he's running on the moon. He simply looks funny, and the guy inside must be a funny guy too, especially if the mascot has helium inside. On the field, he's a buffer between the fans and the team. He creates lightheartedness and joy around the event. You look at him, and you have to laugh. And he's synonymous with the University of Nebraska. In humorous, physical appearance, there's no other mascot like him.[97]

### Stanford's Tree

Stanford University's mascot is the Tree, which also makes it unique. And the Tree gets into a lot of trouble, probably because Stanford students have a reputation for being countercultural. The Stanford Tree does "bad things," inappropriate behavior toward the other team—and it does it all with a smiling face. Why a tree? Stanford's mascot used to be an Indian, but the university dropped that image in the early 1970s due to a student protest over the use of indigenous people as sport mascots. Choosing a totally safe route, university administrators chose cardinal—not the songbird, but the color.

Not able to create a mascot around a color, students held a consensus poll and selected the Tree over other nominated ideas, including a Steaming Manhole and a French Fry. In its first decade, the person inside the Tree was generally a university band managers' girlfriend, but now that (dis?)honorable role goes to a male or female student selected by a Tree Committee during Tree Week when candidates perform grueling, humiliating physical and mental challenges. David Kiefer of Stanford's Office of Sports Information reports that the individual who is selected to be the tree makes the costume, which is why the costumes change each year, and that the tree is not the official Stanford mascot. There is no official Stanford mascot. Rather, the Tree is the mascot of the Stanford band.

"Bizarre and controversial," Wikipedia states, "the Tree regularly appears at the top of Internet 'worst mascot' lists."[98] I disagree. I like the Tree because it's different. And being different, out-of-the-norm, off-the-wall, weird, wacky, and crazy have always been at the foundation of humor.

## THE SAN DIEGO CHICKEN

But the highest tribute of all goes to the San Diego Chicken who was the first on-the-field/court professional sports mascot and, unlike other mascots, is the humorous larger-than-life embodiment of just one performer, Ted Giannoulas. The Godfather of Feathers' first performance came in 1974 as a one-week promotion by a San Diego radio station to give away candy at a zoo. Giannoulas, at that time, was an out-of-work college student at San Diego State University who happened to be in the right place at the right time to get the gig, which paid two dollars an hour.

But Giannoulas saw an opportunity. He volunteered to attend San Diego Padres baseball games as the radio station's beaked ambassador, an unprecedented endeavor. He ran onto the field during time-outs. Later, he would do the same at college and professional basketball games—at a time when there was no time-out entertainment and, unbelievably by today's standards, fans stared at an empty court while players huddled on the sidelines. Giannoulas also pioneered the playing of popular recorded music in the era when stadium organs were the standard musical bill of fare.

In the nearly three decades since, this Jester among the Jerseys has performed live in front of more sixty million people at more than 8,500 games and twice as many total events in numerous nations and all fifty U.S. states. He entertained in Grand Rapids, Michigan, when my sons, Andrew and Kevan, played there for the Whitecaps, a Detroit Tiger minor league team. He's been interviewed on national television, stood on stage with U.S. presidents, and enlivened the acts of the legends of rock 'n' roll. One night, in 1976, Elvis Presley actually stopped in the middle of a song, doubled over in hysteria, at The Chicken's in-the-aisle antics.

As a vaudevillian, The Chicken has been called "the Sir Lawrence Olivier of mascots" and compared to Harpo Marx, Peter Sellers, and Andy Kaufman. But, unlike the pros and actors on screen or stage, Giannoulas performs without a script, with an amateur make-do supporting cast, at impromptu times, and in a venue dedicated to another event—the competition of two teams.

Costumed in a colorful orange body with long, yellow hair, sunset-gold beak, oversized blue eyelashes, a dark blue crown, and webbed feet that look like old-fashioned baseball mitts, this Funny Bone of Humor is an irreverent character whose antics peck fun at umpires, referees, and players. Amazingly, he has never missed an event due to illness or injury, and he is more quietly renowned and respected for his long-standing tradition of signing autographs after each event, sometimes for hours, even in extremely hot temperatures. Giannoulas estimates that more than two million fans have received his signature.

The *Sporting News* editors have named Giannoulas as one of The Top Most Powerful People in Sports of the 20th Century, putting him in the same league with Muhammad Ali, Babe Ruth, Jesse Owens, Pete Rozelle, Ted Turner, and Wayne Gretzky. The Chicken, according to his own pat-myself-on-the-back website, "has reached icon status as a sports and entertainment personality throughout the nation and the world."[99]

His purpose is entertainment, to make people laugh, and he does—he's bad, and he's funny. I have images of the San Diego Chicken strutting up the aisle at a Catholic Mass. He would, no doubt, make fun of the priest. And I have to admit that I would laugh, but there would be others who would consider his antics as unholy. Perhaps. But I bet that the Laughing Jesus would at least crack a smile.

BOX SCORE:

How do you define your sense of humor? How would others?

Do you move through situations with ease and grace? Does your (foul) humor separate you from other people? Or does your (good) humor bring you and others together?

Can you create a solution where there appears to be none?

Do you see why laughter sounds like flowing water, why we relate tranquility and calm with the humorous sound of a babbling brook or gurgling stream?

See yourself in that raft floating down a river. Let go of the oars and allow yourself to go with the flow. How do you feel?

Who are you favorite mascots, and why?

# Education
## "to draw forth"
## (self-exploration)

**Education (ej-oo-kay-shuhn)**

*noun:*

the action or process of educating or being educated; a field of study dealing with methods of teaching and learning.[100]

*I cannot teach anybody anything, I can only make them think.*

—Socrates

*Education is what remains after one has forgotten everything he learned in school.*

—Albert Einstein

As an educator—and all coaches are educators—I love the word *education*. Its significance first came to my awareness through educator, author, and spiritual teacher Parker Palmer in his book *To Know as We Are Known: Education as a Spiritual Journey.*

The current paradigm in American education—and not Palmer's paradigm—is that teachers are to impart information to the students.

But this creates a situation where the focus of education is on testing students to see if they have retained that information. The controlling factor is an inoperable government standard that no child be left behind.

In contrast, Palmer defines education as the act of drawing forth inherent knowledge from both the students and the teacher.[101] And in order to draw forth knowledge, we tell stories. This paradigm corresponds with the ancient wisdom epitomized by the world's great philosophers, such as Socrates and Aristotle who met with their students under the great Greek trees to discuss all that is. Likewise, the world's greatest spiritual philosophers, Jesus, Mohammad, the Buddha, Lao Tzu, and others spoke in stories and parables. Aesop knew the value of educating through fables. The Brothers Grimm evoked fairy tales of universal messages. And the great educators of our day, the many who work with our preschool and kindergarten students, read simple tales and then elicit more stories from the children.

Education, then, is a sharing of stories. Palmer's definition reminded me of this and allowed me, as a teacher and coach, to check my ego at the door. He reminded me that it's my job to inspire and motivate students and student-athletes to find meaning in this experience of education.

I also saw the parallel between scholastic education and religion; both are a sharing of stories. We can neither educate nor worship without stories. As clergy, philosophers, and educators know, drawing forth stories from students teaches us to further our skills as educators and as human/spiritual beings.

This is so evident in sport. In practice sessions, I and my staff give information and show technique. Each contest, then, is a test to see how much the team learned from the practice. Not just the volleyball skills but what they've learned about themselves, their team, their interaction with the other team, and the power in what all of them are doing and creating on the court. The contests become the benchmark about who and what we are as a team; the contests become a parallel for another day in life. As we draw forth the wisdom and knowledge to compete (work together) in life, we all become supreme educators.

As a collegiate educator, the stories I help create are shared stories. They are stories of each team and each season. Some players participate in those stories for only one season, and some for four. But the Women's Volleyball program at Kalamazoo College is, for me, one big story, the overview story of so many players, events, and episodes. My story is a story of what those young women have drawn forth from me. And the ultimate lesson that I have learned is simply this: I am so fortunate to have been, and continue to be, a part of their stories.

Parker Palmer tells us that education is a spiritual journey. To be a holder of my story and the stories of my student-athletes is a spiritual journey. That's what it is. And it's as simple as that: The wins, the losses, the "aha" moments. These are all anecdotes within the bigger story.

The stories are ongoing. The end of the season or the end of a student-athlete's collegiate career is the prelude to commencement, which, of course, means "to begin." After graduation, many former Kalamazoo College volleyball players have come back to tell me their stories of matriculation, career, marriage, births, and deaths. Those highlights are the golden threads of my story.

My story to other educators is this: Education is very powerful. I want coaches, future coaches, and others to know there is so much more to sport than wins and losses. The crowning jewels are the "aha" moments when the players and team come together to click on the court, when they truly compete for the betterment of themselves and the game. I want people involved in sport to know that sport, whether amateur or professional, whether experienced as a player or a fan, is a career, a way of life.

## Redefining the Word

In the English language today, the word *education* has been given a passive meaning. We talk about "receiving an education" or "giving someone an education" as though it is something done to us by an educator.

Actually, as I elaborated above, the word literally means "to draw forth." This means that our mission as educators is to draw forth what is within our students and our student-athletes rather than simply to instill something of us within them. This paradigm shift turns coaching and teaching upside down. Skill, yes, is a learned behavior and one that can be enhanced with guidance and coaching. But the will, the desire, the enthusiasm, the spirit within each athlete is there already. And it is our task as educators to draw those intangibles forth.

## Play or Not Play

Michelle Cassou and Stewart Cubley in *Life, Paint and Passion* have stated, "To play is to listen to the imperative inner force that wants to take form and be acted out without reason. It is the joyful, spontaneous expression of one's self. The inner force materializes the feeling and perception without planning or effort. That is what play is."[102]

Reading these words, I cannot help but to think of children playing kickball or other favorite schoolyard games. And as I think of some collegiate athletic programs and, then, the pros, I wonder what happened on the way from childhood to adulthood. Yes, there are those at the collegiate and professional level who truly enjoy the game. Derek Jeter, All-Star shortstop and captain of the New York Yankees, and Yankee great Mickey Mantle come to mind. So do Pete Rose and Brett Favre, Joe Namath and my personal "she-ro" and role model, volleyball great, Flo Hyman.

Rose may have a black mark attached to his reputation at the moment because of post-career gambling activities, but when he played, he was a joy to behold. Known as Charlie Hustle with a fiery disposition, Rose drew people to the ballparks just to watch him play. He loved the game, and I want to believe he still does. He may have gotten knocked down, but he perseveres.

Favre, as quarterback most notably for the Green Bay Packers but also for the Atlanta Falcons, New York Jets, and Minnesota Vikings, kept getting knocked down too, but he also kept getting back up. He was like the Energizer Bunny who keeps going and going and going. The length of his career was an astounding twenty years in a profession where the average playing time spans only three-and-a-half to four years.[103]

The same can be said for Namath, the legendary quarterback who played 140 games and led the New York Jets to a 16-7 victory in Super Bowl III over the Baltimore Colts in 1969 in spite of having questionable knees due to a serious injury while playing college ball at the University of Alabama.

Flo Hyman inspired everyone she played with and anyone who ever met her. My coach at the University of Michigan would take us to any venue where Flo and her USA National Team were competing within the Midwest. A three-time All-American at Houston and captain of the 1984 Silver Medal-winning U.S. Women's Olympic team, Flo died of aortic dissection caused by Marfan Syndrome during a match in Japan in 1986. When she passed, the entire volleyball community mourned this 6'5" gentle giant of a woman who succeeded in bringing volleyball into the hearts and minds of thousands around the globe.

You can see the spirit of the schoolyard in the way these grown men and women have drawn forth their passion to play, the way they have educated themselves to the real spirit of sport. Consider, for example, Derek Jeter in game three of the 2001 American League Division Series in which the Yankees were playing the Oakland Athletics. Late in the game, a throw from the Yankee right fielder sailed over the head of the cut-off man at first base and was about to die in foul territory between first and home, a situation that would have allowed an extra run to score. But out of seemingly nowhere, there was Jeter, grabbing the slowly rolling ball with his glove and flipping it with the same hand to the catcher, Jorge Posada, who tagged out the runner Jeremy Giambi. I remember the announcer lauding Jeter for the effort. The ball was on the other side of the diamond, far away from the shortstop position, but Jeter anticipated what was about to happen and raced, like a kid in a schoolyard, to make the play.

While a national television audience saw that above-normal yet typical schoolyard play, here's a tidbit about Jeter that is known within the Kalamazoo community but may not be known elsewhere. Jeter was born in Pequannock, New Jersey, but came to Kalamazoo, the same community where I've lived since 1982, when he was four. Even though he grew up here and graduated from Kalamazoo Central High School, he spent summers with his grandparents in New Jersey where he developed a passion for the New York Yankees. When he was a boy, he saw himself playing shortstop for the New York Yankees. Yes, boys and girls have dreams of emulating their childhood heroes and winning games with a clutch play at a critical moment. But Jeter also put his dream into writing. Attending a birthday party of a Kalamazoo friend at age twelve, he signed his name on the basement wall along with the other party-goers, but then added these words: *Shortstop, New York Yankees.*

Two generations earlier, the legendary Yankee Mickey Mantle made a similar prediction about his path to stardom. According to Jane Leavy's biography of Mantle, *The Last Boy: Mickey Mantle and the End of America's Childhood,* "There was a time, back in high school, when Mantle idled through fourth-period study hall with a two-page magazine spread devoted to Joltin' Joe [DiMaggio]. He bragged to his classmate Joe Barker, 'I'm going to take his place in center field at Yankee Stadium.' "[104]

How are those for examples of living and manifesting one's spirit!

Unfortunately, schoolyards are also the domain of bullies, a group of mean-spirited youth who are receiving much public attention among educators, counselors, and the general public. Stories involving these young people are not so inspiring and, quite frankly, not so educational for fans of any age: for example, eye gouging by a University of Florida football player; a female soccer player dragging her opponent down by her ponytail; Mike Tyson biting off the ear of his ring opponent, Evander Holyfield.

What images do these athletes' actions set in the mind of our youth? What messages are sent by the actions of officials and administrators when the eye gouger was suspended for only one-half game while the ponytail puller was suspended indefinitely? And what impression do children receive when Tyson seemed to gain as much notoriety as ridicule for his cannibalistic act?

As professional teachers or in-home educators, aka parents, we need to realize that all of these incidents were overnight media sensations, stories accessible to anyone with an Internet connection.

So, let's ask the ultimate question: What can we learn from these stories that will help us better educate all children—and ourselves?

# NCAA Mission

Realizing that the purpose of the National Collegiate Athletic Association is to keep an educational focus regardless of size and even branding of individual sports programs, it might be wise if we, as fans, remind ourselves on a regular basis of the Association's mission statement:

## CORE IDEOLOGY

The NCAA's core ideology consists of two notions: core purpose— the organization's reason for being; and core values—essential and enduring principles that guide an organization.

## CORE PURPOSE

Our purpose is to govern competition in a fair, safe, equitable, and sportsmanlike manner, and to integrate intercollegiate athletics into higher education so that the educational experience of the student-athlete is paramount.

## CORE VALUES

The Association—through its member institutions, conferences and national office staff—shares a belief in and commitment to:

> The collegiate model of athletics in which students participate as an avocation, balancing their academic, social and athletics experiences.

> The highest levels of integrity and sportsmanship.

> The pursuit of excellence in both academics and athletics.

*The supporting role that intercollegiate athletics plays in the higher education mission and in enhancing the sense of community and strengthening the identity of member institutions.*

*An inclusive culture that fosters equitable participation for student-athletes and career opportunities for coaches and administrators from diverse backgrounds.*

*Respect for institutional autonomy and philosophical differences.*

*Presidential leadership of intercollegiate athletics at the campus, conference and national levels.[105]*

# Incorporating Sport

Sport at the professional level and within some big-name collegiate programs has become a major business enterprise. According to revenues reported to the NCAA in the 2004-05 academic year, the University of Georgia had the most profitable athletic program in the nation, earning $23.9 million. The University of Michigan was second at $17.0 million. The University of Kansas was third at $10.1 million. The NCAA figures also show that some major universities lost money, as much as $8.7 million by the University of Arkansas-Little Rock.[106]

The athletic department at the University of Michigan, my alma mater, is a corporation, independent from the university, and the football program there generates enough income to fund several other sport programs that don't draw enough attendance to be profitable. This situation also exists in many other schools, especially the major universities that are eligible to play in post-season bowls. Known as the Bowl Championship Series (BCS) schools, their budgets typify the growing magnitude of athletic budgets. When I played volleyball at the University of Michigan in the late 1970s, for example, we traveled in vans, but with the need for these BCS schools to gain more and more nationwide exposure combined with the effects of Title IX, the current volleyball team flies around the country and competes on a national stage. That's good news for Title IX and the realization of the dreams we had as players "back in the day."

Even the cost of sport facilities is staggering. Joseph McCafferty, writing in *CFO* magazine as editor in chief, reports that, in the late 1990s, "the University of Texas spent $90 million to upgrade and expand the football stadium on its Austin campus."[107] In 2006, the university's board of regents approved another $150 million for further expansion, concluded prior to the 2009 season, that brought the seating capacity to 100,119,[108] making it the largest football venue, by seating capacity, in the State of Texas and the sixth largest stadium in the NCAA.[109]

The University of Michigan recently expanded the seating capacity of its football stadium, known as "The Big House." That project, according to McCafferty's article "The Money Bowl," cost $226 million, making it the largest football stadium in the country, or the "Big-*est* House." Oklahoma State University spent $102 million to upgrade its football stadium in the mid-2000s. McCafferty quotes a University of Texas official as saying, "You've got to have great facilities if you are going to remain competitive."[110]

With these examples in mind and also considering the cost of professional athletes' salaries, including such one-time extravaganzas as a professional boxing match, the rising cost of equipment for athletes at all levels and all ages, cost of promotion and advertising—and we can even throw in the cost of transportation for teams that fly and parents who drive kids to practices and games—I wonder about the total economic impact of sport in our world. While I know that my budget at Kalamazoo College is miniscule in comparison, the apparent truth is that it is impossible to know the total U.S. financial outlay for athletics. Any entity that has such financial impact must also have the ability to shape or change cultural thought.

## The Probability of Becoming a Pro

What does all this spending mean to the kids in school who dream of becoming a professional athlete? In an Internet article on athletic recruiting titled "Estimated Probability of Competing in Athletics Beyond the High School Interscholastic Level," the NCAA reports real numbers for youth who dream of becoming a pro. The bottom-line statistic (in the right-hand column of the following table) shows that less than one-half of one percent of all high school senior athletes will ever don a professional uniform; in most sports, the percentage is less than one-tenth of a percent.

**STUDENT-ATHLETES WHO ADVANCE FROM HIGH SCHOOL TO NCAA TO PROFESSIONAL SPORT (ANNUAL)[111]**

|  | HS Sr. Student Athletes | NCAA Sr. Student Athletes | NCAA Student Athletes Drafted | % HS to Pro |
|---|---|---|---|---|
| Men's Basketball | 155,756 | 3,758 | 44 | 0.03% |
| Women's Basketball | 127,088 | 3,418 | 32 | 0.03% |
| Football | 317,801 | 14,418 | 250 | 0.08% |
| Baseball | 135,195 | 6,626 | 600 | 0.44% |
| Men's Ice Hockey | 10,644 | 911 | 33 | 0.31% |
| Men's Soccer | 21,601 | 4,800 | 76 | 0.07% |

*Note, per NCAA: These percentages are based on estimated data and should be considered approximations of the actual percentages.*

The NCAA's message advises young people to find meaning in sport itself, regardless of the level at which you play, because odds are you're not going pro. The reality is that reaching the pinnacle of success is real only for the few who do it, and it's not realistic for the vast majority of kids playing youth sports.

My sons tried. Both were in the Detroit Tigers farm system when I began to write this book. Now Kevan still is, and Andrew is not. Kevan still believes he can do it, so he's got to find a way to make it real for him. For him, as well as for any aspiring athlete, reaching the majors has to be an unshakable vision, a belief. And that vision has to be so strong that it burns into the psyche as much as Derek Jeter's proclamation on his friend's basement wall as a twelve-year-old burned into his. There has to be opportunity, a route, a path through organized programs, the NCAA, the minor leagues. The days of sandlot ball played by the boys of summer and Cinderella stories of a kid in Iowa or the Projects being scooped up by a scout who happens to observe a pick-up game are gone.

Kevan and Andrew have two parents who are coaches. They heard messages about sport—the true meaning, value, and spirit of sport—on a regular basis. This gave them an edge. They could go into baseball and follow their passion with a knowing, with an education. They could draw forth their own stories, based on their memories of earlier accomplishments, whether in the previous game or a highlight from previous seasons. They knew what was inside of them, and they were drawing that forth too. That was their knowing, their story. And they followed that inherent knowing to get to that level of professional sport. They were among the 0.44 percent of high school kids who get drafted by a major league baseball organization.

If Kevan continues, he will learn what every professional athlete, whether rookie or veteran, knows: It takes a lot of years and work and practice and lucky breaks to become "an overnight success." Stardom, for many, also comes with a cost, especially in sports that characterize big expenditures, high salaries, and intense pressures to perform. "Many pro athletes pay a heavy personal cost," Andrew has told me. "The time away from family, friends, and home takes its toll on relationships."

Andrew was released by the Tigers during spring training in 2010. The news came cold and out of the blue. Jim and I were there in Lakeland, Florida, the day he got the news. So was Kevan, of course. Andrew took it hard. Baseball had been his dream, his story, part of his education. He wanted to play baseball. And he was good—oh, only if he could have pitched with his left hand, the way he writes with his left hand. Later on in the summer, he got an offer to play in the farm system for the Philadelphia Phillies, but by that time, he had begun a new life outside of sport with a job he enjoyed and had set a date to be married to the love of his life, who he had dated for five years.

He gave baseball a shot, and baseball gave him a shot. But ultimately it was a lifestyle that he experienced for a while but then came to realize he really didn't want. Part of education is in knowing when to write a new story. That's what Andrew is doing now. And so is Kevan. Every time he takes the mound, he writes another new chapter.

## Educating for Meditation

I had the opportunity to attend a retreat at the Fetzer Institute in Kalamazoo during the winter of 2005. Fetzer's mission at that time was beginning to include bringing love and compassion into higher education, so they gathered representatives from campuses across the country whose missions and programming reflected these issues. There, I met Ed Sarath from the University of Michigan who taught a class entitled Jazz 450 through the School of Music.

The class sounded fascinating because of its focus on music, rhythm, and intentional meditation. As a matter of fact, students needed to meditate and journal on a regular basis as part of their homework for the class. I mentioned to Ed that I thought this concept would benefit athletes. He agreed and said that he actually prefers to have athletes in the class. He said that centered, conscious players perform at a higher level.

It may have been coincidence, but I was counseled as a very young student that "there is no such thing as coincidence," so I chose to believe that hearing this message was meant to benefit our family. I called Andrew, who was a student at U of M at the time and told him to immediately sign up for the class. He ended up taking it during his senior year and admitted that the meditative skill did, indeed, help him center and focus when he took the mound.

The following year, as Chair of the Physical Education Department at Kalamazoo College, I created a meditation class and had it added to our curriculum. The reason: Physical Education is not necessarily only about teaching students how to raise their heart rates, sweat, stretch, and play. Rather, one of the most valuable skills for wellness, success, and accessing happiness lies in the ability to quiet our minds and thoughts, and this must begin with conscious awareness of meditation's benefits. The class has been a success and fills quickly on a regular basis. That is true education—drawing forth what is inside the student, drawing forth what the student brings to the moment.

## Drawing Forth Integrity

In yet another so-called "physical" education lesson during one of my volleyball classes, I found a preponderance of students breaking one of the cardinal rules of volleyball: not to make contact with the net during play. When I asked them about it, and asked them to call their own net faults, I was told, "Other teams do it during intramurals so we have to, too."

I wondered aloud what might happen if my students called faults on themselves regardless of what the other teams were doing. Would that lead their opponents to do the same? And would that bring a higher level of integrity to the game? "No," they said. "They (the other intramural teams) want to win, so they will still do it," implying that the only way to win is by breaking the rules. Being an educator, I replied that bringing a greater level of integrity to the games may *not* serve the opponent, but it *will* serve us. And I sincerely hoped that, in saying that, I was drawing forth their inherent integrity.

During that term, the city of Kalamazoo hosted the USA Curling Nationals, which I attended. Imagine my delight to see "The Spirit of Curling," the organization's mission statement for self-regulating conduct within their sport printed on the first page of the event program. I shared this with the volleyball class, and to my delight during our competition, all were calling their own faults with honorable conduct:

## THE SPIRIT OF CURLING

Curling is a game of skill and of traditions. A shot well executed is a delight to see and so, too, it is a fine thing to observe the time-honoured traditions of curling being applied in the true spirit of the game. Curlers play to win but never to humble their opponents. A true curler would prefer to lose rather than win unfairly.

A good curler never attempts to distract an opponent or otherwise prevent him from playing his best. No curler ever deliberately breaks a rule of the game or any of its traditions. But, if he should do so inadvertently and be aware of it, he is the first to divulge the breach.

While the main object of the game of curling is to determine the relative skill of the players, the spirit of the game demands good sportsmanship, kindly feeling and honourable conduct. This spirit should influence both the interpretation and application of the rules of the game and also the conduct of all participants on and off the Ice.[112]

# "Why We Play"

In *Tales from the Small Time,* author Jim Moore tells stories of the combination of athletic and scholastic achievement among NCAA Division III student-athletes. At this level of play, these young women and men do not receive scholarships based on athletic skill or accomplishment alone. Rather, they compete for scholarship dollars from the same pool of funds as all other students at the institution. The criterion that determines if they receive financial aid is based on factors such as academic prowess, leadership, service, and extracurricular pursuits.[113]

Their decision to play on a Division III athletic team is an indication that they are honestly in school for an education, and they play because they love the game. It also means that, because of their level of commitment to a team, they are persons filled with courage and perseverance as they overcome the odds of balancing time between classes, studying, practice, and games. They are true student-athletes.

The same passion that led Jim Moore to write *Tales from the Small Time* led me to create a campus-wide academic/athletic event called "Why We Play." For years at Kalamazoo College, I knew sport was much more than a game for our student-athletes. At the same time, I had a strong desire to alter what I saw as a situation of polar opposites.

The city of Kalamazoo is situated on glacial moraines deposited during the most recent Ice Age, and the topography of Kalamazoo College's campus is rolling. The chapel and most classrooms are, literally, "up the hill," and the athletic facilities are "down the hill." As I served in my two positions as associate chaplain up the hill and a coach down the hill, I wrestled with what I saw as little connection, even disociation and imbalance, between the two realms within this academic community.

Therefore, I had a desire to create a public arena for the athletes to tell their stories and to present themselves as passionate, eloquent, fun, and yet very serious students. But, in addition or as a requisite for telling their stories to others, I wanted them to consider the collegiate life they had chosen and, indeed, ask themselves *why* do I play?

By seriously asking this question, these students discovered, as I believed they would, that the spiritual life is a purposeful life, and the sportual life is a purposeful—*and playful*—life. Therefore, these students moved beyond often typical reasons for playing a sport initially: because their friend plays or because their parents think they should or because they will get a trophy at the end of the season. These students literally play for love of the game and for the educational value they receive. By crafting their stories, these student-athletes came to realize that sport is an activity for them to access their greatest self. And by telling their stories to their peers and faculty, they are figuratively leveling the college's academic and athletic landscape.

For these reasons, "Why We Play" has become an annual event, part of Kalamazoo College's Chapel program. Each program—held in fall or winter of the academic year in the idyllic chapel at the top of the hill, shaded by tall oak trees—features four or five student-athletes who stand before their academic peers and faculty to, in many cases, bare their souls. The entire program consists of introductions, music of some sort, the student-athlete speakers, and an athletic alumni speaker. And each year, the chapel is filled with an audience of two hundred to three hundred people. "Why We Play" is not only proof of the power of storytelling; it has become a manifestation of one of the defining tenets of Division III colleges.

## NCAA DIVISION III PHILOSOPHY STATEMENT

That primary tenet is found in the opening sentence of the NCAA Division III Philosophy Statement: "place the highest priority on the overall quality of the educational experience and the successful completion of all students' academic programs." The second sentence contains words that speak to me as a coach: "to establish and maintain an environment . . . in which coaches play a significant role as educators."[114] When I read these words, I feel that the NCAA is accomplishing the same objectives we do with the "Why We Play" program at K College; we are not only leveling the topography between sport and academics but we are realizing the necessary balance between the two.

I can also see how this code might be applied in different ways and for different purposes by the administrators and students on various campuses. On some, like at Kalamazoo College, the traditional emphasis has been on academics with athletics being a secondary calling, and on other campuses, especially at the Division I BCS schools, it seems that sport is the calling card that also draws students to receive an academic education at that institution.

Regardless of perspective, I think that all educators at all scholastic levels, from early childhood through post-graduate programs, whether coaches, teachers, professors, academicians, or parents, can benefit from reading and following the principles of this Division III Philosophy Statement:

Colleges and universities in Division III place highest priority on the overall quality of the educational experience and on the successful completion of all students' academic programs. They seek to establish and maintain an environment in which a student-athlete's athletics activities are conducted as an integral part of the student-athlete's educational experience, and in which coaches play a significant role as educators. They also seek to establish and maintain an environment that values cultural diversity and gender equity among their student-athletes and athletics staff. To achieve this end, Division III institutions:

(a) Place special importance on the impact of athletics on the participants rather than on the spectators and place greater emphasis on the internal constituency (e.g., students, alumni, institutional personnel) than on the general public and its entertainment needs;

(b) Shall not award financial aid to any student on the basis of athletics leadership, ability, participation or performance;

(c) Encourage the development of sportsmanship and positive societal attitudes in all constituents, including student-athletes, coaches, administrative personnel and spectators;

(d) Encourage participation by maximizing the number and variety of athletics opportunities for their students;

(e) Assure that the actions of coaches and administrators exhibit fairness, openness and honesty in their relationships with student-athletes;

(f) Assure that athletics participants are not treated differently from other members of the student body;

(g) Assure that athletics programs support the institution's educational mission by financing, staffing and controlling the programs through the same general procedures as other departments of the institution. Further, the administration of an institution's athletics program (e.g., hiring, compensation, professional development, certification of coaches) should be integrated into the campus culture and educational mission;

(h) Assure that athletics recruitment complies with established institutional policies and procedures applicable to the admission process;

(i) Assure that academic performance of student-athletes is, at a minimum, consistent with that of the general student body;

(j) Assure that admission policies for student-athletes comply with policies and procedures applicable to the general student body;

(k) Provide equitable athletics opportunities for males and females and give equal emphasis to men's and women's sports;

(l) Support ethnic and gender diversity for all constituents;

(m) Give primary emphasis to regional in-season competition and conference championships; and

(n) Support student-athletes in their efforts to reach high levels of athletics performance, which may include opportunities for participation in national championships, by providing all teams with adequate facilities, competent coaching and appropriate competitive opportunities.[115]

# "What Will They Say This Year?"

Most liberal arts college curricula demand about forty hours per week for in-class and expected out-of-class work, which translates into having a full-time job. The NCAA allows twenty hours per week for in-season practices, which, in terms of total hours, is like working overtime. If an athlete wants to sleep, eat, and maintain healthy relationships (and have clean laundry), there is little time left for anything else, specifically during the season. Therefore, sport becomes a defining part of a collegiate athlete's life, scholarship or not. Indeed, an education becomes the joyful, spontaneous expression of one's true self.

Over the course of several years of listening to "Why We Play" stories on an annual basis, our student body and faculty have been moved to both laughter and tears, through sorrow and into joy. If there is one emotion that runs through the service each year, it is joy. Joy bubbles up and spills out the chapel doors. It rolls across the lawn and around the stately oak trees, into the dormitories and classrooms, and down the hill to the athletic venues and offices.

In the first year of "Why We Play," we were blessed to have future pastor Jevon Caldwell-Gross, the men's basketball team's point guard, as the "clean-up hitter," the fourth and last person to speak. At the conclusion of his remarks, there was not a dry eye in the house. Passion, purpose, team, love, sacrifice were all a part of Jevon's storied messages, and now in his post-collegiate role as pastor, he inspires from the pulpit of a church rather than as captain of a team.

Word spread. In future years, more athletes came forth to tell their stories. "Why We Play" became the arena I hoped it would become. It was a place where all athletes could gather with their learning community and share what had been our little secret down in the Athletic Department: "We've found *joy,* and it lives in *us!*" And every year, "Why We Play" became the Chapel of choice. Even students linked to athletics in the most casual way began to wonder and ask, "What will they say this year?"

As the convener of the speakers, I would first ask the coaches if they would recommend anyone with a story. Then I would ask the athletes themselves, "Do you want to tell your story?" But, as the tradition grew, underclass athletes would approach me either immediately after the service or sometime during the year and say that they wanted to speak at next year's "Why We Play."

At first, we recorded the athletes' stories on audio tape. Then we advanced to video. And now we edit the stories into a professional-quality presentation and post them online for all to see.

When all is said and done, education—both academically and athletically—is a spiritual pursuit, and no one says it better on our Kalamazoo College campus than those who are fed by the ins and outs of competition on a daily basis—our student-athletes.

---

**TIME-OUT:**

Go to http://vimeo.com/kzooathletics to see video of some of the "Why We Play" services at Kalamazoo College.

---

## Superstar (Self) Educators

The "Why We Play" program on March 6, 2009, was a transformative service, to be sure. Three hundred students, faculty, and administrators filed in to the campus sanctuary, anticipating. All who were slated to present were seniors. And each one spoke like a superstar that day.

Holly, the first speaker, was unique. Holly was not an athlete, but she certainly participated in athletics—and sportuality. During her four years at Kalamazoo, Holly volunteered to sing the National Anthem prior to almost every athletic contest. Her support of each of our athletic teams was unwavering, even through some pretty victory-lean years. After her comments at "Why We Play," however, the weight of the losses seemed to fade, and everyone sat up a bit straighter. She related that singing the National Anthem at K College games even came into play in one medical school interview when the interviewers asked her to actually sing it for them. She was accepted! After telling this story, Holly sang "The Star-Spangled Banner" one more time in the college's sacred chapel space, acknowledged by thunderous applause.

The next speaker was Sarah who, through four women's soccer seasons and several injuries, led the team. Because of her great leadership ability, she was elected as president of the Athletic Leadership Council of the student body at the college. Not only did Sarah sacrifice on the field, she spent two years creating community among athletes and non-athletes.

The next speaker was not someone I selected but someone who my selectee, Allison, asked to speak in her stead. For seventeen years, one team—not Kalamazoo College—dominated cross-country in our conference, but, finally, in the fall of 2008, the women's champion hailed from another school: ours. And that person was Allison. In asking her to speak, I intended that she would tell the story of being a conference champion and a national contender. Being humble, however, she deferred to her teammate Jillian, a fantastic runner and, as it turned out, a very thoughtful and humorous speaker. First acknowledging Allison as her friend and praising her accomplishments, Jillian went on to tell how running was in her blood. Standing no higher than the podium, she joked about her ancestor's height challenge; that they had to learn to run simply to survive. She continued on with her joy in the sport, concluding with "endorphins are like crack for healthy people."

Our men's swim team has long been an inspirational bunch. Along with their success in the pool, all of our swimmers inspire many on campus with their abilities in the classroom despite the two-a-day practices that begin at 5:30 a.m., commonly known as "0-dark-30." Taking the audience in his hands with confidence and humor, Ryan spoke of his "brothers" on the team, the glue that holds them together, and how he considers the pool to be one of his greatest classrooms, without GPA as a standard of measure.

One of the most difficult times in any sport is dealing with pain and injury. The next speaker, Lindsay, from women's tennis, spoke with emotion, truth, and passion about her knee pain, surgery, rehabilitations, and desire to play and help her team. Lindsay left no doubt through her tears that hers had been a long, but rewarding, journey. Each heart in that room felt her pain and, hopefully, helped diminish it.

Steve then followed as a dual-sport athlete in both football and baseball, waxing eloquently about the sacrifices he and his teammates made on a daily basis to train, practice, and play. He also had been through three surgeries as a collegiate athlete, but rehabilitated each one and moved forward with his teams—and trainers—at his side. Steve is the guy you want on your team. He is selfless, positive, persevering, with good humor and a smile that lights up the room. "Where else would you have seventy-five guys show up at your father's funeral?" he asked. Probably at several places, but here at Kalamazoo College, it made a world of difference to a grieving twenty-year-old man.

In recent years, we have begun to include an alumni athlete in the program. I find that this historical perspective provides an element of mentored wisdom and validates all the experiences of our current student-athletes, and then relates wisdom gained along the way. Jeremy Cole had graduated in 1995 and was arguably one of the best men's basketball players ever to wear a Hornet jersey. A recipient of the prestigious NCAA post-graduate scholarship, Jeremy used it to attend Notre Dame's School of Law. And today within his law firm in Chicago, he is currently far, far away from his glory days as an athlete. However, he spoke about the lessons of winning and losing and how they created "the best classroom" during his undergraduate education. Now a successful attorney, Jeremy honors the game, the team, the coaches, and the experience that helped shape his life. His is a story of why we *continue* to play.

Every year is like that. Sportuality creates the service. Joy is the result.

BOX SCORE: Write your "Why We Play" story. If you were asked to speak at next year's service, what would you want to put out there to your peers and colleagues about your experiences in sport? Where is your meaning and purpose?

As an athlete or a fan, who are/were your best educators—other than yourself, of course? Did they allow your real self to shine?

As a coach, how do you work with your athletes to bring out their best? Are you an educated athlete, coach, or parent?

How do you feel about professional salaries, given the knowledge that early legends of sport and the women of the All-American Girls Professional Baseball League and members of the Negro Leagues were compensated so minimally? What does it say about our national priorities when we compare current professional salaries to the average salary of an educator?

Write a letter to a favorite coach or educator who may not know the difference they made in your life.

# FOURTH QUARTER:
## Religion, Holy, Sanctuary, Sacrifice

# Religion
## "to link back, to connect"
## (purpose of man-made institutions)

**Religion (re-li-jen)**

*noun:*

a set of beliefs concerning the cause, nature, and purpose of the universe, especially when viewing the creation as the work of a superhuman agent (God); devotional and ritual observances often containing a moral code to govern the conduct of human affairs; a specific fundamental set of beliefs and practices generally agreed upon by a number of persons or sects such as the Christian religion, the Jewish religion, and the Muslim religion; the body of persons who adhere to a particular set of beliefs and practices; something one believes in and follows devotedly; a point or matter of ethics or conscience; Archaic: strict faithfulness or devotion; Idiom: to "get religion" is to acquire a deep conviction of the validity of religious beliefs and practices or to mend one's errant ways.[116]

*It is easy enough to be friendly to one's friends. But to befriend the one who regards himself as your enemy is the quintessence of true religion. The other is mere business.*

*—Mohandas Gandhi*

*True religion is real living; living with all one's soul, with all one's goodness and righteousness.*

—Albert Einstein

*Religion is to do right. It is to love, it is to serve, it is to think, it is to be humble.*

—Ralph Waldo Emerson

I grew up in a divided household where my mom was a practicing Episcopalian and my dad a Catholic. Because they had married in the Catholic church, they had made a vow to raise their children according to the tenets of that religion. However, they didn't say *not* to include my mother's Episcopalian religious practices in the mix. So I spent my childhood believing it was normal for members of a family to attend two different churches and two different religious education classes and that Sunday breakfast was the *real* ceremony that united us before our family went off to our separate worship spaces: Mom to the Episcopal church; Dad and us kids to the Catholic church. It was not unusual, though, for my brothers and me to attend Mom's church when Dad was unavailable and to do the religious education classes in *both* places. It is no wonder that I found meaning and solace in being involved in athletics as a member of team and in a form unlike my religion, which allowed me, as a female of the 1960s and 1970s, to participate fully.

## Redefining the Word

In its original Latin and, later, in Middle English of the twelfth century, *religion* meant "conscientiousness and piety." Today, many people might not consider those two words to be synonymous, but by looking at their roots, we can see they are. Piety means "devoutness and dutifulness in religion, fidelity to natural obligations." To be conscientious means "to be guided by one's sense of right and wrong, to be scrupulous, honorable, honest, upright, and just."

Consider these words in the context of community that was already defined in an earlier chapter: "a body of people living in the same place under the same laws; society at large." When we consider the communities in which we are involved—familial, societal, religious, or that of the natural world—we see that we are, indeed, conscious, and we practice dutifulness to our community and fidelity to our natural obligations within those communities. We act according to our sense of right or wrong, and this is as true for both contemplative monks and charitable nuns as it is for members of violent gangs.

In whatever community we belong and participate, we have certain ties that fasten and bind us to our group. And that realization leads us back to the original Latin definition of *religion* where the root word is the verb *religare,* which means "to tie, fasten, or bind." Interestingly, *religare* is the root for ligament, a band of tough tissue that holds bones together or supports an organ. In sport, one of the most common and debilitating injuries is a torn ligament that causes bones, often the knee, to become no longer held in place by the body's own natural forces.

Religion is also the human practice that provides a structure through which we know our Creator or the original thought of our being, to know as we are known, to seek the One, to be whole, to be healed, to know peace.

British political writer David Edwards in his book, *Burning All Illusions,* summarized all of these concepts when he wrote: "Religare means to rejoin, to link back the individual with society, the world and the cosmos. This fundamental meaning of religion has nothing to do with a personal god, theology or dogma. It is, above all, a term that implies coherent connection, a connection that doesn't necessarily imply a priestly intercessor."[117]

# Spirit, Spirituality, and Religion

Previously, I've mentioned my role as a Eucharistic minister within the practice of my Catholic faith. Likewise, I think it is necessary to distinguish my views on the relationship between religion and spirituality and then link both to spirit.

Spirit is an animating or vital principle—breath—that gives life to physical organisms. Spirituality is the quality or act of being spiritual. And religion is a set of beliefs concerning the cause, nature, and purpose of the universe, especially when viewing the creation as the work of a superhuman agent, God.

But what's the connection between these three?

Spirit is an essential part of our inner, supernatural being; it is the breath by which we live, our human soul, our divine connection to the Holy Spirit, our ethereal energy that we bring to the teams we join and the games we play.

We cannot see spirit, but we can see and witness the practice of religion and spirituality. We practice for games, often with a team or at least a coach. We practice religion with a congregation as well as a spiritual coach: a priest, rabbi, minister, imam, shaman, or other member of the world's clergy, regardless of name or denomination. Therefore, religion and spirituality are physical manifestations of our invisible spirit, just as drifting sand or waves on a lake or leaves fluttering on a tree are the physical manifestations of an invisible wind.

Wayne Teasdale, in his book *The Mystic Heart,* explains:

> Religion and spirituality are not mutually exclusive, but there is a very real difference. The term spirituality refers to an individual's solitary search for and discovery of the absolute or the divine. It involves direct mystical experience of God, or realization of vast awareness, as in Buddhism. Spirituality carries with it a conviction that the transcendent is real, and it requires some sort of spiritual practice that acts as a catalyst to inner change and growth. It is primarily personal, but also has a social dimension. Spirituality, like religion, derives from mysticism.[118]

My religious and spiritual practices tell me that my life is beyond understanding; it is steeped in the mysticism that Teasdale describes. But for me both my religion and my spirituality become real—manifested—with sport. I see the physicality of spirit on courts and on courses, in pools and in arenas as I compete or watch others compete. I see that spirit connects us to the eternal One who is also the center of belief by those who practice both religious rites and spiritual ways of living.

The practice of sport is comparable to the practice of religion. We arrive at our arena or court at an appointed time, just as when we attend a religious service on a scheduled day at a specified time. We focus on the ball, the catch, the goal in the same way that we focus on a prayer, a ceremony, a Eucharist. Likewise, the practice of sport is comparable to spiritual practitioners who focus on the breath when meditating.

The Bible implores us to "pray without ceasing,"[119] which means that God is instructing us to make our very life a prayer. Our practice becomes a prayer. Our interaction with our teammates becomes a prayer. Our game becomes a prayer. Our encounter with the teams with whom we compete becomes a prayer. That is the essence of spirit, the essence of breath, whether relaxed or heavy with exhalations magnified through physical exertion.

When we recognize our participation in sport as an act of spirituality and religion, we then realize that we can use sport as a catalyst for change toward a more peaceful, more divine, more spirit-oriented world. Wayne Teasdale's words that previously helped define *Spirit* in that chapter are also applicable here: "By allowing inward change, while at the same time simplifying our external life, spirituality serves as our greatest single resource for changing our centuries-old trajectory of violence and division. Spirituality is profoundly transformative when it inspires in us the attitude of surrender to the mystery in which we live, move, and have our being."[120]

His closing words—"live, move, and have our being"—are found in the Bible, the book upon which the Christian religion is set: "For in Him, we live and move and have our being."[121]

Through sportuality, can we transform from divisive violence to a greater connectivity with all and the One? Can we really learn and understand that competition means to work *with* and not *against?* I believe we can. I believe that, through sport, we can move away from war-focused thinking and action toward the inner peace promised by all religions.

# Origins of Religion

In the previous chapter on Education, I drew a parallel between education and religion, stating "both are a sharing of stories." That concept is worth repeating here in this chapter on religion. Consider that, in all probability, humankind's first stories were both religious and educational. We know our forebears studied the movement of animals and the edibility of plants, and they observed the moon and stars and weather. These served as the foundation of both their early education and their belief in a divine spirit, the key components of their very culture, which they conveyed through stories and cave-wall art. Eventually, these stories grew in stature and the cryptic drawings evolved into icons and jewelry and ceremony to create and sustain religious societies.

A census was recently released telling that, as a nation, the people of the United States are becoming less religious and more secular. That being the case, what then is filling our religious void? How are we demonstrating and manifesting our meaning and purpose? How are we defining our lives?

Do the difficulties we face in life reflect this lack of meaning, this searching for truth?

Does sport fill a part of that void in our culture?

In *The Mystic Heart*, Wayne Teasdale tells us, "We need religion, yet we need contact with the divine, or ultimate mystery, even more. Religions are valuable carriers of the tradition within a community, but they must not be allowed to choke out the spirit, which breathes where it will."[122]

Joseph Chilton Pearce, in his Introduction to *The Death of Religion and the Rebirth of Spirit*, states, "As culture is a major plank in our ideation, religion is a major plank in our culture, and it, too, is on the wane, which has given rise to fundamentalism as a political-cultural force."[123] A passage on the book's dust jacket mentions world violence, which I believe also includes violence affirmed within the culture of sport:

> We are all too aware of the endless variety of cruel and violent behavior reported to us in the media,

reminding us daily that in every corner of the world someone is suffering or dying at the hands of another. We have to ask: Is this violence and cruelty endemic to our nature? Are we at our foundation, really so murderous? . . . Pearce, a lifelong advocate of human potential, sounds an emphatic and convincing no. . . . Pearce shows us that if we allow the intelligence of the heart to take hold and flourish, we can reverse this unconscious loss of our true nature.[124]

Pearce emphasizes this point within the text: "Joy and pleasure are the bricks and mortar of physical, psychological, social, and spiritual development, and the developing brain must experience joy and pleasure if the complex integration of sensations is to take place."[125]

To repeat and emphasize, the word religion comes from the Latin *religio* meaning "to tie back, reconnect, relate again to something of the past." The origins of religion may lie in humanity's early attempts to link again with the primal bond of life that had been broken by divisive elements within culture, such as greed or hoarding due to a sense or misperception of scarcity.

In his book *From Season to Season: Sports as American Religion*, Joseph L. Price takes the stance that sports, while not Christian, Buddhist, Muslim, Jewish, or Taoist, can indeed take on the characteristics of and, for some, even be a form of popular religion because they teach religious qualities of heart and soul, and that "through their symbols and rituals, sports provide occasions for experiencing a sense of ultimacy and from prompting personal transformation."[126]

If we consider the wide-reaching effect of sport on our life as well, it is on a parallel with religion as a political-cultural force. Examples include President Obama filling in the bracket for the NCAA basketball tournament; worldwide broadcasts of major sporting events like the Super Bowl, the Olympics, the NBA finals, baseball's World Series, or World Cup Soccer; the enormous economic impact of sport on our culture; and even team names such as Angels, Saints, and, yes, Blue Devils.

Sport also reinforces cultural stereotypes that have been the basis of religious conflict, cultural violence, and unhealthy practices within unhealthy nations. As Pearce writes:

> War is a direct cultural effect.... As it is a sure bet that an individual will speak French if born and brought up in a French-speaking family and community, so will culture cast its far more powerful generic influence on those born to it. Culture as a field effect functions much like language acquisition: it results in spontaneous, imitative learning below the limen of our awareness.[127]

We only need to look at examples of team branding to see the effect of sport cultures built on violence or subjugation of another: the Fighting Irish, the Fighting Illini, and many numerous team names and mascots that depict Native American Indians.[128] Perhaps the awareness and decreasing number of team names that depict Native Americans is a reflection of our cultural awakening to the greater impact of sport on our common psyche.

If we can count on culture to shape belief and behavior, can sport, as a cultural plank, also have far-reaching effects? Can sport be a factor to help create peace? Can sport help us culturally define peace as the union, the link, the *religare* of self with the Creator where peace and joy are linked?

I continue to believe in the power of sport to transform our culture, our beliefs, our behaviors. Sportuality rises again.

## The Trinity—in Religion, in Sport

Three is a golden number, and the concept of "three" or "threefold" appears in various forms in many languages: *triad* in Latin and Greek, *triune* in Latin, *trinitat* in German, *trindod* in Welsh, and *trionnoid* in Irish, to name a few.

In physics, a three-sided object or three points create three dimensions of height, width, and depth. In architecture, a triangle embodies solidity and strength. This is why photographers and surveyors use a tripod, a stand with three legs, to hold their cameras and scopes steady. It is why pyramids and geodesic domes comprise an assembly of unilateral triangles.

In human relations, the nuclear family consists of a mother, father, and children. And in times of dispute, a plaintiff and a defendant will seek resolution through the aid of a third party, such as an arbiter, mediator, or judge. Trinities are also found in human physiology and psychology in the mind/body/spirit connection. Even in literature, poets and writers use a phrase of three—such as, dog, cat, and mouse; sun, moon, and stars; and faith, hope, and charity—to add meaning, depth, and richness to their work. And Native Americans honored a trinity of Mother Earth, Father Sky, and Grandmother Moon through which they found harmony, balance, and wholeness.

Among the world's major religions, the heart of Christian doctrine is based on three components of God—the Father, the Son, and the Holy Spirit—commonly known as the Holy Trinity.

The Hindu religion recognizes Shiva and Vishnu as *Mah‾adevas*, the "great gods" who, along with Brahma comprise the *Trimurti*,[129] also known as the Hindu Triad or the Great Trinity, this threesome represents the three aspects of God—creator, maintainer or preserver, and destroyer or transformer.[130]

The Jewish faith presents a host of trinities: The Torah's three books, the Torah, the Prophets, and the Writings. The Mishna's three parts, Talmud (learning), *halakhot* (daily Jewish laws), and *haggadot* (history). The patriarchs are Abraham, Isaac, and Jacob. The mediators are Miriam, Moses, and Aaron. Prayers are spoken in the morning, afternoon, and evening. Israel consists of priests, Levites, and Israelites. The name Moses in Hebrew is written in three letters, as is his tribe of Levi. In an Internet article titled "The Trinity Is Jewish," author Rachmiel Frydland writes, "God has made everything and arranged everything in a Trinitarian way. . . . God, Himself, is a Trinity. . . . Savior, Messiah, and Son of God."[131]

Threesomes also abound in sport: three contacts in volleyball; three-point shot in basketball; three-point field goal in football; three periods in hockey; three strikes in a row in bowling is a "turkey" and considered a feat of skill for average amateur bowlers; three strikes for an out and three outs per inning in baseball, where the most common double-play combination involves three players, shortstop, second baseman, and first baseman. And in horse racing, the trifecta is a perfect prediction of who finishes first, second, and third.

By adopting a Trinitarian concept, we can rid ourselves of the duality of winning and losing and, thus, elevate the game to the deific universality exemplified by the Trinity. Perhaps in sport, the trinity is expressed as God the Sport, God the Game, and God the Competitors (which includes the coaches, cheerleaders, and fans).

Additionally, several authors have explored the relationship between sport and religion, some having done so from a civil religion perspective and others as reflections of Christianity. The following passage from Craig A. Forney's *The Holy Trinity of American Sports: Civil Religion in Football, Baseball and Basketball* talks about "the big three" seasons as a religious calendar of sorts:

> Together, the three sports produce a daily way of life, a never-ending connection to the national worldview, pivoting on acts of devotion to the spoken and written word. At special points of the week, game action inspires the gathering of individuals . . . in a show of common faith in a team.[132]

This idea is the embodiment of the trinity as part of the American civil religion; it creates a religious environment that is based on the values and beliefs of the country. As a woman, of course, this is somewhat disconcerting, acknowledging the "big three" as a civil religion, but it does reflect a belief in a male dominated religious paradigm, and therefore a male God. Perhaps Title IX, which at its core is intended to establish equality within education, through sport can "trickle-up" to include religions as more women involve themselves in athletic competition.

Mystic, prophet, and spiritual traveler Meister Eckhart (1260-1329) believed that the spiritual journey is a spiral path, ever growing and expanding, eventually leading us back to our starting point, our beginning, our Creator. His reflection on the Trinity, to me, is perfect for this idea of play, of humor and laughter, and of purpose in sport:

*Do you want to know what goes on in the core of the*
*Trinity?*
*I will tell you.*
*In the core of the Trinity*
*The Father laughs and gives birth to the Son.*
*The Son laughs back at the Father*
*And gives birth to the Spirit.*
*The whole Trinity laughs and gives birth to us.*[133]

The trinity is the perfect double play as embodied in the historical threesome of Chicago Cubs' shortstop Joe Tinker, second baseman Johnny Evers, and first baseman Frank Chance, who were immortalized in the poem "Baseball's Sad Lexicon" by New York Giants fan Franklin Pierce Adams in 1910.

*These are the saddest of possible words:*
*"Tinker to Evers to Chance."*
*Trio of bear cubs, and fleeter than birds,*
*Tinker and Evers and Chance.*
*Ruthlessly pricking our gonfalon bubble,*
*Making a Giant hit into a double—*
*Words that are heavy with nothing but trouble:*
*"Tinker to Evers to Chance."*[134]

The trinity is the perfect play in volleyball: pass, set, spike. And the pitcher's dream: one, two, three strikes, and you're out.

Eventually the trinity represents our whole being: mind/body/spirit.

We do ourselves a disservice when we focus on only one aspect of a game, a player, or a religion. Teasdale reminds us of the "tripartite dialogue" of the head, heart, and hands, at least one of which is necessary for commitment to an interspiritual community. The head is the academic, intellectual level, abstract and concerned with principles and beliefs. The heart represents a shared spiritual practice. And the hands represent the fruit of head and heart, building trust through a common goal, task, or concern: an issue of peace, justice, or collaborative project. To me, the tripartite dialogue sounds a whole lot like sport, with our mutual commitment to each other and our interspiritual communities and teams.

## Sport: Religion or Civil Religion?

Civil religion is a term that describes certain fundamental beliefs, values, holidays, and rituals within a culture that may parallel or be independent from the practices of various church-based religions found within that culture.

Sociologist Robert Bellah first coined the term in 1966 after having studied decades of previous observations by several prominent scholars. Bellah stated, "While some have argued that Christianity is the national faith . . . few have realized that there actually exists alongside . . . the churches an elaborate and well-institutionalized civil religion in America."[135]

For examples of civil religion practices in sport, consider that collegiate coaches at all levels in the U.S. make an annual pilgrimage to national conventions, some of them coordinated to occur at the time of national championship games. Think of fans who gather around the back of an SUV (an altar) for a tailgate party, consisting of food, drinks, and camaraderie. Think of friends who gather in someone's home for pizza and beer (a communion) to watch the "big game" in any sport. Think about crowds of people who express their nationalistic civil religions in bars and pubs (community) to watch large-screen telecasts of professional soccer matches in many European, African, and South American nations. The NFL has for years scheduled their contests on Sunday, the Christian Sabbath. For better or for worse, millions of Americans connect to "The One" via the professional football community.

Picture the many, many major motion pictures and documentaries that have been made about sport heroes, real or imaginary, of any age, from *The Mighty Ducks* to *The Babe Ruth Story*. We've even made movies of temporary or would-be heroes, such as *Cool Runnings*, which was inspired by the Jamaican bobsled team mentioned earlier. Look at the numerous books that have been written about the legends of the games, those who excelled in their sport as well as those, like

Jackie Robinson, who helped change the paradigms of American civil religion.

To honor our heroes, we retire numbers and hang their jerseys, as well as other memorabilia, in halls of fame. We erect larger-than-life statues in our ballparks and stadiums. In Detroit, a twenty-four-foot-long bronze arm and fist commemorates the career of boxing legend Joe Lewis and the nearby arena is named after him. How refreshing is that, especially in an era when corporate money is attempting to buy their way into our civil religion by paying for stadiums onto which they can attach their names rather than preserve the names of historical greats as we once did with Wrigley Field (named for William Wrigley, Jr., owner of the Cubs) and Briggs Stadium (after then Tigers owner, Walter Briggs)?

All of these icons and rituals are examples of how we have made sport into a civil religion. We are playing with our bodies what we cannot speak with our words—the unspeakable becomes the game.

Neale Donald Walsch, in *Conversations with God, Book 1,* relays this idea on religion: "Religion is your attempt to speak the unspeakable."[136] Such as attempting to describe the trinity. Sometimes, the best we can do is *do* the unspeakable. When we are engaged sportually in a game, there are no words to describe it—it's not good, it's not bad, it simply *is*.

Andrew didn't have all these authors, publications, and studies in mind when he wrote in his Easter blog:

> I usually don't like to blend baseball and religion. I think that each is sacred in its own right and usually one is used to amend the deeds done by the other (I think we all know which the first is there). But when you think about the similarities and how each can be used in life, baseball and religion are not so different. That home run, by the way, probably restored some Detroit fans' faith in religion again, because I'm sure the words "Thank you, God" were uttered throughout.

Andrew simply knew of the transcendent, transformative power of sport to reconnect us with the One.

Prayer exists within every religious tradition. In going through the effects from my mother-in-law's house after her death, I came upon a framed black-and-white photo of my husband pitching for his high school in the state championship game, with the following prayer by an unknown author on yellowed newsprint taped to the glass:

> O, Lord, you who asked that the little children be allowed to come to You, look with special kindness on this little pitcher. Keep his arm strong, his eye sharp. In Your infinite wisdom, let him understand that winning isn't always better than losing and help him learn to accept both graciously. And, Lord, if you can help him keep the ball down and away from time to time, I know he'd appreciate it. I know that in the grand scheme of things, it's not a major consideration, but it's awfully important to him. He's a good little boy, Lord, and he always looks so lonely out there.

Funny, I am now praying like that for my sons. In this act, I am linked to my husband's late mother and her hopes and dreams for her son. Linked—with the ties and bonds of mothers' love. In a state of religion—*re-ligio*—where we both speak our prayers and do our sport.

---

BOX SCORE: If you accept and understand the concepts of this chapter, you have some belief in the transformative power of sport. How does your belief fit with your traditional religious paradigm? How do you feel connected to the Creator because of your sport activity?

# Holy
## "to become One"
## (purpose of evolution)

**Holy (ho-lee)**

*adjective:*

worthy of absolute devotion; sacred; having a divine quality[137]

*In every community, there is work to be done. In every nation, there are wounds to heal. In every heart, there is the power to do it.*

—Marianne Williamson

*Joy is the holy fire that keeps our purpose warm and our intelligence aglow.*

—Helen Keller

To make something holy means to make it complete, whole; to be uninjured and healthy. In ancient times, this was considered to be a good omen. (Well, I guess so.)

My career has been not only coaching but teaching the idea of being whole, healthy, and healed to the general student body at Kalamazoo College. My teams understand this; they've created a trinity of thought with the words: focus, finish, believe. In order to focus and finish, a person must be whole in heart, mind, body, and spirit. Putting the concept of believing into this trinity creates a mindful, Mobius loop that doubles back on itself. When a person or team believes in themselves, they are able to focus on and finish any task, and as they focus and when they finish, they increase their belief in their ability to focus on and finish the next task. That is a holy state—the state of holiness, the state of wholeness. Because I don't separate what I do when coaching from what I do when teaching, regardless of the venue, my career has been whole and holy.

In my office, I have a dish that is as symbolic to me as any chalice, grail, or arc of a covenant to a religious community. The ceramic dish was given to me in the 1980s by a softball player at Kalamazoo College. Toby had had migraine headaches, and I used my knowledge of health and healing to teach her techniques through which she healed. In her gratitude, she made the ceramic dish in an art class at the college.

The dish itself is a memory treasure, but over the years I've added more memories—gifts from other athletes and students that signify the wholeness I find in education and in sport. There's a tiny volleyball and a fortune cookie fortune that reads, "In order to win, you have to participate." There are engraved stones that remind me of holy moments: one has an image of a heart, another has the word "connections," a third says "teamwork," and a fourth advises "let go and let God." A painted stone reads "K Volleyball 2004," a gift from that team. All of these sit atop sand from the beach where the 2004 team spent some practice time.

For both Toby and for me, this dish is an affirmation of that healing time. It's a re-*mind*-er for me to keep my mind into healing, into making my life more whole, into making myself more holy.

## Redefining the Word

Generally accepted today as a synonym for hallowed, blessed, sanctified, or consecrated, the word *holy* actually has an etymological link with the health and wellness of the human body. And because the body is an athlete's number one tool, holy has a direct connection to sport.

The word originated in Old English as meaning "wholeness or being whole, sound, or well." The meaning evolved in other languages to mean "of good omen or uninjured," a desired condition for any athlete or team, and "hale and healthy." The connection with holy or sacred, no doubt, came about because ancient people revered the body as the way of expressing the soul and because a healthy body is able to hunt and gather food as well as participate in physical games, such as tribal contests and ancient olympics.

# Inspiring Holy Oneness

Lou Gehrig, the "Pride of the Yankees," stands in front of a microphone at home plate. Yankee Stadium is filled with admiring fans. He addresses them, "Fans," and the word echoes throughout the stands: Fans ... Fans ... Fans ... "I consider myself the luckiest man on the face of this earth." He speaks of his seventeen-year-career, the baseball men he's been associated with, his mother-in-law, parents, and wife. He concludes, "I may have had a tough break, but I have an awful lot to live for."[138]

The tough break of which Gehrig spoke was the motor neuron disease, amyotrophic lateral sclerosis (ALS), which became named after him—Lou Gehrig's Disease—because of his love of sport and his relationship with millions of people whom he touched with humility and gratitude.

Yet this direct connection between such a great athlete and a physical ailment establishes an irony that seems to be common to sport. In metaphysics, disease is considered to be a disconnection, a state of being in which the affected person is not at ease, or in a state of dis-ease, the opposite of being at ease. Metaphysically, dis-ease is linked with an imbalance of mind, body, and spirit.

Now, I'm not saying that Lou Gehrig's physical illness came from him being out of balance. Rather, I want to honor this great man and great player while also showing the connection between wholeness, health, and sport—and how all are directly related to a healthy culture.

A healthy culture on the team indicates wholeness, a result of members having been inspired to and having done the work of bonding, that is, coming together in mind, body, and spirit. This is the theory that HeartMath identifies as occurring when all are in coherence with others. Recall the Three Musketeers and their famous tenet: "All for one, and one for all" as they parried with their dueling rapiers against nefarious foes.

Gehrig alluded to this oneness in his speech when he said, "I have been in ballparks for seventeen years and have never received anything but kindness and encouragement." He spoke of oneness when he talked of "everybody down to the groundskeepers and those boys in white coats remember you with trophies." He glorified oneness when he complimented his "wonderful mother-in-law," his "father and mother who work all their lives so you can have an education and build your body," and his "wife who has been a tower of strength and shown more courage than you dreamed existed."[139] These words make holy the healthy culture of Gehrig's professional and home life.

This high level of oneness is a fundamental part of healthy individuals and healthy teams; it is at the core of champions. Oneness appears in all areas of equestrian, for example, where horse and rider must totally synchronize, and in auto racing, where the driver must completely feel the car's every nuance for mechanical failure or danger as well as have a sixth sense about potential contact with other cars while traveling inches apart at speeds of over 100 miles per hour.

But even though many, if not most, athletes seek ways to manifest wholeness within themselves and through their inner spirit, dysfunctional and unhealthy practices have become an unacceptable norm within sport, causing cynicism in regard to great physical prowess. For example, "He must be on steroids" is a common comment that detracts from a performance rather than inspiring awe.

# Drugs that Defeat the Mind, Body, and Spirit

Rather than investing the necessary years to become a success, some players are using performance-enhancement drugs to short circuit that process. In actuality, they are short circuiting themselves and potentially their careers, their glory, their fame, and their health. They are also short circuiting our culture's healthy and wholesome view of sport.

The use of drugs and stimulants is a false belief that an external substance can enhance physical well-being and performance; it is an erroneous understanding that the external substance is more powerful than the healthy, holy, inner self. Drugs are an affront to the very spirit and inherent wholeness of an individual and society.

Dr. John Underwood, who spoke to students at Kalamazoo College in October 2010, reports, for example, on the impact of alcohol, even a couple of beers, on athletic performance. His research at the Lake Placid Olympic Training Center focuses on "Pure Performance" and substance use on the brain and central nervous system. Dr. Underwood's research has been partially inspired by the life and death of collegiate teammate Steve Prefontaine, a great runner in the 1960s and 1970s who died in a car accident on the way home from a party. "More than four beers at one sitting can affect performance for up to ninety-six hours," says Underwood, "eclipsing the previously held belief in 'the forty-eight-hour rule,' which says that drinking is okay forty-eight hours outside of competition."[140]

I believe that healing comes at a higher, more spiritual level than can ever be attained, at least over the long term, through artificial chemicals, whether they are depressants or stimulants. But because sport is a paramount physical manifestation of the body—and because our culture has allowed and even encouraged the use of drugs to enhance results—those substances have pervaded sport and bastardized pure performance and pure competition. As a result, society now questions superior athleticism, especially record-breaking achievements. "How did he, she, or they do that?" society asks. "Did they use performance-enhancing drugs?"

The drugs available to athletes—professional, amateur, collegiate, and in high school—are numerous and plentiful: illicit street drugs; prescription diuretics, beta-2 antagonists, beta blockers, anabolic steroids, peptide hormones; over-the-counter items such as alcohol, caffeine, and other stimulants; and masking agents that hide the presence of the others in blood or urine tests.

Drug testing originated in professional sport but is now common even in high schools, an indication that our culture accepts cheating as the only way to gain fame and fortune within sport. Ultimately, though, the responsibility for wholeness and healthfulness must reside with each athlete who will, hopefully, ask, "What good is a championship if it is tarnished by deceit? What is the value of a home run record or the most touchdowns or the fastest time or the highest/farthest jump if the accomplishment is subject to suspicion?"

Surely, no *true* athlete can value a medal if it is won with the aid of illicit means. But it happens. And when it does, the athletes have not only let themselves down, but they have betrayed and made cynics of those who are desperate for heroes, especially the impressionable young, the future superstars and heroes of sport.

To have a healthy sport attitude, players at any age and level must realize: The body can wear a medal; the mind can believe it won a medal; but the knowing part of that human trinity, the spirit, will suffer as a result of the untruth. The ultimate calamity is to the abusing individual, the misaligned, out-of-sync self.

So what is to be done? What is the secret to attaining holiness—healthfulness—in sport? What is the cultural cure for drug abuse among athletes? Is testing the answer? I think not. Cultural change doesn't come from a chemical kit; the kit is only fuel for more abuse and more cynicism. Cultural change originates from within, from an attitude of holiness and reverence for mind and spirit.

I realize this thought flies in the face of the long-standing—but becoming outdated—paradigm of what we know of modern, Western medicine. Oftentimes, we medicate a malady away or surgically repair it—the scalpel or the pill. That fits the cultural belief of our society, that we can impose an external substance or invasive procedure to create super humans and superhuman performance. But the Six-Million-Dollar (or Six-*Billion*-Dollar, with inflation) Man or Woman is an illusion.

Surgery and drugs may be physical realities in that we can see the knife cut the skin and tissue, and we can hold pills and vials and injection needles in our hands. But when we use drugs to enhance performance, we create the illusion that the enhanced performance is real. And at the core of our being, both as individuals and society, we know it's not real. That's why we test—we test to catch the culprits. But the solution, the real solution, comes from within and the power of our individual holy, healthy, whole spirit. This is where we as coaches, athletes, parents, and fans can utilize sport to inspire ourselves and the youth of our society to a truer, higher performance.

## Unsanctified Heroes

Unfortunately, the lure of fame has pervaded sport, and many—too many—athletes have been found out and exposed to scandal. Some have been suspended, lost medals, and had awards taken away. Some have been deprived of entry into a hall of fame.

Here is a summary of notable examples, as ranked in an Internet article titled "Drugs & Sport" by CBC Sports Online:

1. In the 1970s and '80s, the East German government gave performance-enhancing steroids to thousands of amateur athletes, which resulted in that country winning many more Olympic medals than before. Athletes said they thought they were taking vitamins.

2. After the 1983 Pan Am Games, nineteen athletes failed to pass drug tests, Canadian weightlifter Guy Greavette and teammate Michel Viau were stripped of medals after testing positive for steroids, a dozen American athletes withdrew, and athletes from other countries left without explanation.

3. In what is considered the biggest doping cover-up in sport, nineteen U.S. athletes were allowed to compete in Olympic Games from 1988 to 2000 even though they had failed drug tests.

4. After testing positive for anabolic steroids, Canadian Ben Johnson was stripped of his gold medal and world record and banned from competition for two years after winning

the 100-meter sprint in record time of 9.79 seconds at the 1988 Olympics.

5.  Starting in 1995, Irish swimmer Michelle Smith, previously a mediocre Olympian, avoided drug tests then suspiciously won three gold medals and one bronze in the Olympic Games in 1996. A forced test in 1998 revealed an impossibly high level of alcohol content, an indication of an attempt to alter her specimen with liquor, and Smith was suspended from competition for four years.

6.  China, previously not a swimming powerhouse, won four swimming gold medals at the 1992 Olympics and twelve at the 1994 world championships. Eleven athletes tested positive for dihydrotestosterone at the 1994 Asian Games, and over forty Chinese swimmers since 1990 have failed drug tests. Four swimmers left the team prior to the 2000 Olympics due to suspicious drug test results.

7.  At the Tour de France in 1967, Britain's Tim Simpson died after riders began to use amphetamines and alcohol to gain a competitive edge in the 1960s. In the late 1990s through mid 2000s, riders, including national champions, failed drug tests and admitted to the use of various performance-enhancing drugs or masking agents.

8.  Professional baseball's questionable heroes include Mark McGwire, who hit a record-breaking seventy home runs in 1998, Barry Bonds, who beat McGwire's record in 2001 and holds the record for most homers in a career [762], sluggers Jose Conseco and Jason Giambi, and MVP Ken Caminiti, [who died of a drug overdose in 2004].

9.  The International Olympic Committee disqualified two non-medalist members and banned two officials of the Austrian Nordic cross-country team after the 2002 Olympic Games, and six Finnish skiers tested positive for

banned substances at the 2001 world championships in Finland.

10. Starting in the early 1990s, Nandrolone, a banned steroid, has been the subject of hundreds of doping cases among athletes in many sports, especially track and field, cycling, soccer, and tennis. [141]

Not mentioned in this list, but up for inclusion are Lance Armstrong, the winningest Tour de France rider ever, who has repeatedly been the subject of scrutiny for alleged drug use and blood doping, and seven-time Cy Young Award-winning pitcher Roger Clemens who denied using steroids and HGH.

# What Does Government Have to Do with It?

When Marion Jones won five track and field medals at the 2000 Summer Olympics in Sydney, Australia, she was on steroids. She admitted this in 2007 while also acknowledging that she had lied to the press, sports agencies, and two government grand juries when she earlier denied her usage of performance-enhancing drugs. One of those grand juries had been impaneled to investigate BALCO, a "designer steroid" later associated with major league baseball player and home run king Barry Bonds and others. In October 2001, Jones pled guilty to the charges, accepted a two-year suspension from track and field events, and then immediately retired from competition. She also forfeited all medals, results, points, and prizes obtained after September 1, 2000, and she served six months in jail in 2008 for perjury.[142]

In August 2010, major league pitcher and seven-time Cy Young Award winner Roger Clemens was indicted by a federal grand jury for allegedly lying to Congress about his use of performance-enhancing drugs. The indictment stated that Clemens obstructed a congressional inquiry when he made fifteen different statements while under oath that included denials he had ever used steroids or human growth hormones. Clemens maintained his innocence before and after the indictment. He had volunteered to appear before Congress to clear his name of the drug abuse charges on or off the field, and an article at CBS News online on August 19, 2010, quoted his attorney as saying, "Roger is looking forward to his day in court."[143]

What these two stories have in common, and what makes them different from the scandals listed in the previous section, is the role of the U.S. government to investigate the use of illegal substances by professional and amateur athletes.

Technically, some of the performance-enhancing substances are not illegal under the law. Many of them are available from pharmacies with a doctor's prescription. Beta-2 antagonists, for example, increase oxygenation in the body and are often prescribed for asthma patients. Beta-blockers help prevent heart attack, hypertension, and other heart conditions. Caffeine is available in tablets, tobacco, coffee, and many soft drinks. And alcohol can be purchased in any bar or liquor store. However, these substances are banned within the self-regulating world of sport when they are used to enhance individual performance. They are frowned upon by fans who realize that the players who use these substances may have cheated by ingesting or injecting substances that helped them break records held by loved and admired long-ago heroes who set the standards of their respective games on pure prowess alone.

So, the question arises: What does the government have to do with the use of banned substances within sport? Is Congress just one more unsanctified hero? Or do legislators have a legitimate right to investigate?

Robert Longley, a staff writer for the U.S. Government Info page posted by About.com, a part of The New York Times Company, posed the question this way: "Did the House Government Reform Committee have the authority to hold its much-reported hearings into steroid use in Major League Baseball, or was the testimony of several former and present MLB stars little more than a taxpayer-funded photo-op?"

Longley says the original committee, known as the Committee on Government Operations, was established in 1927 to investigate "the operations of Government activities at all levels with a view of determining their economy and efficiency." Over the years, the committee's powers have grown to that of being "Congress' chief investigative and oversight committee." Leaning toward the "photo-op" answer, Longley points out that the committee's role is "the investigation and reform of the operations of the government itself." And "the use of steroids by professional baseball players clearly does not fall under the scope of their authority."

But then Longley delivers an on-the-other-hand point of view, which states that the Committee has "the authority to conduct hearings on any subject falling under the jurisdiction of Congress." One such subject is the Federally Controlled Substances Act, which, he writes, "regulates the use of performance-enhancing drugs, including steroids." The Committee's jurisdiction also relates to Major League Baseball's exemption to federal anti-trust laws that link to a precedent-setting case in 1922 regarding the right of a team to move from one city to another.

Longley's conclusion is, "While its exemption from anti-trust laws has nothing to do with steroid use by players, it does place the affairs of Major League Baseball squarely under the jurisdiction of Congress."[144]

In my opinion, Congress probably means well. After all, baseball is America's national pastime, and it's facing a national breakdown. But Congressional intervention as well as the infusion of billions of advertising dollars from corporate sponsors, the exorbitant price of player salaries, and what seems to be a greater concern—among some players—about individual statistics than simply playing the game are all external influences that are eroding the fans' trust in sport.

And what happens if our trust in baseball, or any sport, erodes? The media blasts the players, agents, and owners. Fans find other pastimes. The money flow decreases. Advertisers lose interest. The sport itself loses—or evolves. That is, the players who sought glory through illicit means realize that their glory is fleeting and fleeing, if not taken away from them. And players who simply want to play the game emerge; like cream, they rise to the top.

Perhaps that is why minor league baseball, both in the farm systems and the independent leagues, is gaining popularity. For a fraction of the cost of a major league ticket, you can take your family to a real old-fashioned game that's a true joy to watch. The players might not be major league quality, but they certainly show as much spirit as

Pete Rose, "Charlie Hustle." In minor league parks, players are more accessible for autographs. Some owners let kids run the bases after every game, and post-game fireworks become a picnic as families toss blankets on the outfield grass to sit and watch, rather than racing to get out of the parking lot.

While I believe it is good that Congress is paying attention to America's national pastime, I also think the true resolution to unnatural external intervention is the spirit within fans and athletes themselves. While some push, use, condone, and cover up the use of banned substances, I believe that there are enough others who express their true spirit that sport, in its pure, wholesome, holy form, will prevail.

## Perfectly Peaceful, Holy Sport

And then there's volleyball.

Volleyball has been called a "peaceful sport." As a matter of fact, since the beginning of the Peace Day campaign in Afghanistan's eastern region in 2009, the Sub-Directorate of Youth of Nangarhar, in coordination with the Youth Association, has organized several volleyball and cricket matches among the youth. Because there is no physical contact between the teams, the rules only require a team to make the ball hit the floor in bounds on the opponent's side of the net. Achieving this requires intense teamwork, as though a team be in a six-person dance. It requires a team to be coherent, to be all on the same page, as described with the introduction of HeartMath in the chapter on Community.

When I first heard about HeartMath in 2002, I did the math. If, indeed, the human heart rate rhythm can be measured six feet away from the body, and if there are six people in a thirty-foot by thirty-foot area, there must be some sort of heart-to-heart influence happening on a regular basis out there on the court. There *had* to be more to being a team than everybody donning the same uniform. Players need to be whole, healthy, healed, and, yes, holy—in their hearts.

I believe coaching volleyball demands that we honor all parts of the game. We must pay attention to the physical skills of jumping, swinging, passing, setting, and hitting. We must be mentally aware of the tactics involved: how to score, how to use our lineups effectively, how to observe the opponent's tactics and tendencies. But volleyball also demands an acute spiritual awareness because of the close proximity of the players and their shared goals. Players affect one another greatly, and if we are aware of this and can consciously practice it as consciously as we practice our attack or our defense, we will have much more success.

Think about your particular sport, whether you play, coach, or spectate, and the possibilities for it to become a more whole—and holy—experience as you become more aware of these connections.

# The Holy Zone

This is what my team is doing. We're getting there. We want to be that team who plays *in the zone* and knows when we are in the zone, whether in practice or in a match, on the court and off.

The zone exists in volleyball as much as any sport. You can see and feel those times when the opponent seems to hit everything directly at you for an easy return and when every ball you hit scores. Even the language we use to teach concepts can make a difference—can create this holy zone—if we understand this and know the language to use. For example, on defense, a player might think or say "make the ball come to me" rather than "I have to go to the ball." While it might appear to the onlooker that the defender is pursuing the ball, the change in thought puts the defender in charge and actually in a better position to play the ball. This occurs because the defender removes fear-based thinking, the dread of not being able to reach the ball, stop the attack, and thus lose the point.

Culturally, our entertainment, our media, and even our national alert system would have us believe that we are always surrounded by unknown attackers whom we must fear. Who said that Martians are enemies and want to dominate us if they *would* land on Earth? The entertainment industry did, with special credit to Orson Wells and his (in)famous radio drama *War of the Worlds*. Who would have us believe that nature is our enemy? The news media, which, for example, continued to highlight the devastation of the Gulf Coast after Hurricane Katrina, and even weather personalities who describe sunshine as good and rain or clouds as bad even though both are necessary and holy gifts from God. Who would have U.S. citizens be constantly aware of danger from people in other nations? The Homeland Security Department, which frequently announces airport messages such as "Today's security alert is orange."

Anywhere in sport, you may have a story of the *holy zone*. You *know* this story because you are either on a holy-zone team or you play against such a team. If you are on this team, you know what having "it" is like. And if you play against them and have never experienced the "it," you have probably wondered what is the "it" that they have. Maybe you scratch your head in dismay because, by comparing your team's athletic abilities, stats, and all physical indicators, your victory should be a given—on paper, that is. But beyond the odds makers' predictions and what appears like a certain "should be," the underdog's victory is the stuff of upsets and championships and even legends. That's why we play the games.

When playing in the holy zone, the winning team is completely whole. Those unexpected outcomes constitute the unforgettable holy moments of sport. They create a feeling that really never leaves. And some sort of cultural transformation happens because what is supposed to be "just a game" transcends to something much higher, more holy, more blessed, more sacrosanct. The players involved become more revered, and even the game site seems to be sanctified and consecrated in some way.

Take, for example, the inspired play of the New Orleans Saints' win in Super Bowl XLIV in February 2010, a win that represented a moral victory for all the people of New Orleans and Louisiana. Those aptly named Saints, on that day, persevered, overcame odds, maintained focus, stayed strong, and *knew* that the hearts of a city, wounded and suffering from Hurricane Katrina, were in their hands. What a moment. An indescribable holy, sportual moment!

Consider also Armando Galarraga of the Detroit Tigers when he threw a perfect game on June 2, 2010. Except he wasn't credited with a perfect game, and you won't find a record of it in the record books.

Why? Because, on what would have been the last out of the game, umpire Jim Joyce made the incorrect call. The ball had been hit to the Tigers first baseman, Miguel Cabrera, who flipped an underhand toss to Galarraga, covering first base. In a play practiced endlessly during spring training and throughout the year, Armando beat the runner to the bag by a step-and-a-half. Jim Joyce was steps away from Galarraga, with his hands stretched wide, palms toward the ground—the sign for safe. What did Galarraga do? He smiled. Sure, it was a smile of disbelief, a smile of "you've got to be kidding." But, of course, the umpire wasn't kidding, the call was made, and it would forever stand even though he apologized later to Galarraga, the Tigers, and to all of baseball that he had made a mistake. Again, what a moment. Galarraga could have been angry, he could have blown his top, he could have flung his cap or glove to the ground in disgust. But, instead, he smiled, went back to the mound and quickly went about his business of retiring the next batter. The game may not be recorded as a perfect game, but Galarraga certainly was a perfect, holy gentleman and professional on that day. And the game—the game of baseball—and all of sport are better because of his performance after "the call."

# Holy Influences

A metaphorical image states that one bad apple can spoil the entire barrel, and it's true. With apples, the solution is to pull out the bad apple and remove its rotting (rotten) influence from the remainder of the apples. But those are drastic measures for a team of humans. Yes, a player can be pulled from a game or even suspended from play for a period of time. But because our minds are cognitive and not fodder for applesauce, memories linger and continue to influence.

Take the image of your six volleyball players on the court or imagine any team that must share a playing field, a locker room, or a travel bus. See one of them with a negative attitude. Place that image inside yourself. Think about how you, as one individual, can influence your teammates.

See how the foul player—carrying a negative thought or belief, in a bad mood, with an evil intent, holding on to nonforgiveness, or experiencing a lack of love—can emanate negativity from one moment to the next. See how that thought in the mind can exhaust you and your team's entire body system with fear, stress, anxiety, misery, depression, illness, and death.

In contrast, see how one team player—carrying a positive thought or belief, being a cheerful spirit, and exhibiting generosity, kindness, forgiveness, love, peace, harmony, fellowship, calmness, and joy—can emanate positivity and joy. See how that thought in the mind can lift you and your team's entire body system up out of the doldrums and into a realm of higher consciousness, greater physical health, more positive mental well-being, and more abundant existence than what you might possibly imagine.

It is said that Jesus did four things while on Earth: He taught, fed, forgave, and healed. Healing is the stuff of the holy zone, created by the holy influences that raise sport and athleticism to its highest, holiest, most whole, and most healthy potential.

---

**BOX SCORE:**

Do you feel holier, that is, more whole, more complete, healthier, and more alive in your total mind, body, and spirit when you are involved in some way with sport? What are your experiences with drug use in sport and how do you feel about it? Have you ever experienced "The Zone" during training or competition? Have you watched it as an observer? Consider and write about this experience, this feeling.

# Sanctuary
## "to honor our holy places"
## (purpose of place/space)

**Sanctuary (sank-chu-wer-ee)**

*noun:*

sacred space; a holy place, such as a building set aside for worship
of the divinity or of one or more deities; a consecrated place, such as
the part of a church where the altar is placed.[145]

*All of the places of our lives are sanctuaries; some of them just happen to
have steeples. And all of the people in our lives are saints; it is just that
some of them have day jobs and most will never have feast days named
for them.*

—Robert Benson

Recall the meaning of sacred to mean holy, whole, healed ... to realize
the One. The gym was always a place where I felt whole and wholly
healed. But not until years later, during the dog days of our preseason
when I was standing in the middle of the empty gym at Kalamazoo
College, did this hit me: the nets, the lights, the movement of the air,
the stale smell of old sweat, the sweet smell of new leather volleyballs,
the ritual. I felt the juxtaposition of silence and noise, dark and light,

action and inaction. Yes, I can turn on the lights, but the team lights up the gym.

I belong in this place where I feel joy, this arena of sport to which I have been called, this sanctuary that feeds my soul.

## Redefining the Word

A sanctuary, by modern definition, is related to a church. A holy place, by modern definition, is related to a spiritual practice, to a site of an ancient apparition, or to sanctified ground. If you ask most people if they think of a sports stadium or arena or a court or field as a sanctuary or a holy place, you will probably receive a strange look in return.

As we've seen in the previous chapter, holy refers to being whole, healed, and healthy. Does that concept not apply to a locker room or a gym or any workout facility? In a training room, you will find an athletic trainer who will help you be healthier; you will have access to instruments and salves to heal your wounds. In a gym, you will find machines, free weights, workout mats, and other tools to help you become stronger. On a field of play, you will experience physical exertion to help you balance your body and mind with the mental rigors of a desk job.

The word *sanctuary* comes from the Late Latin and Middle English word *sanctuarium,* which is a combined form of *sanctus* and *arium* or *ary. Sanctus* is a Latin word that means "holy or hallowed."

Well, we've already discussed holy, but can you think of any place in sport that is hallowed territory? How about the red zone on a football field? The circle on a wrestling mat? Or the key on a basketball court? What about the green in golf . . . or the goal crease or the goal in hockey? Or any goal or way of scoring, such as a finish line, goal line, hoop . . . home plate. My sons have found the bullpen to be a sanctuary as part of their pitching careers. And anyone who has been on any team can tell you that the locker room is sacred, from the junior high cement benches between rusting metal lockers to the luxuries of professional clubhouses.

Sanctuary, in religious terms, also applies to places where ritual occurs. Again, think of ritual in sport: the coin toss at the start of a football game, the toss-up at the start of a basketball game, the throwing out of the first pitch and standing for a seventh-inning stretch at a baseball game, leading a winning horse to the winner's circle to receive a wreath, the victory lap in auto racing, the presentation of a cup or trophy at the end of a championship season, or the appearance of Olympic athletes on a dais to receive medals amidst the playing of the gold medalist's national anthem. Are these not ceremony and ritual—as sacred to sport and fulfilling to the action of athletics as is ceremony within a church? Even the annual player drafts in professional sports and the announcements of star high school players regarding the college of their choice are rites of passage that equate to any religious sacrament of confirmation.

These ceremonies of sport are populated with congregations of fans, clergy in the form of coaches, righteous patriarchs in the form of umpires and referees, and media who sing players' praises as gloriously as any choir intones hosanna and alleluia.

Which is more sacred in your eye: a cathedral in your religious denomination or a hall of fame for your favorite sport? For me, as a Catholic with a love for baseball, it's quite easy, actually, to see similarities between Cooperstown and the Vatican. I revere both.

Here are other parallels:

Religion has martyrs. Sport has fallen heroes.

Religion honors saints. Sport enshrines superstars into halls of fame.

Religion has scriptures. Sport has rule books.

Religion has vestments. Sport has uniforms and jerseys.

Religion has statuary and icons. Sport has statuary and icons—as well as retired numbers.

Religion has relics. Sport has memorabilia.

Religion has ancient churches, some of them modern and some of them in disrepair. Sport has stadiums, arenas, courts, and tracks, some of them newly built and some from bygone eras that are settling into oblivion or have already crumpled under the weight of a wrecking ball.

The point is that a sanctuary is any place where holy moments happen, where community comes together to experience the same thing at the same time, where a common message is heard. There is power in shared ritual, whether at Mecca or around the eighteenth hole of the Masters Tournament in Augusta, Georgia.

A sanctuary is any place we hold in high regard, any place where we find fulfillment, any place where we identify with our whole and holy, healthy self.

## Confirmation

Conrad Kottak was the professor for my introductory anthropology class at the University of Michigan. Being an undergraduate in my first anthropology class, I was unfamiliar with his fame, but I did know he wrote our textbook, *Anthropology: The Exploration of Human Diversity*, which introduced me to new ideas and cultures and which must have been effective because I can recall it thirty years later. Dr. Kottak presented an idea that then struck me as most unusual: that, in our culture, McDonald's restaurants were like church. There was ritual, dialogue, and exchange of money. And to make it more real for me, the picture of McDonald's restaurant in the textbook was the very one where I was employed at that time. The building was as unique as Ann Arbor, Michigan, a community rich in progressive thought and culture as it was to the generally conservative surrounding Midwest. It was a two-story brick structure with stained glass windows. It really *did* remind one of a church![146]

This idea seared into my mind like hamburgers on the grill, and every time I visit any fast food restaurant, Conrad's words "*Mac-Donald's*," with the emphasis on Mac, comes back to me.

Sports and their venues have the same effect. With this recollection, I contacted my former professor thirty years later to see if he had more information on holy or sacred venues. One day later, I received a reply with more than that; he sent me entire chapters about sport, about purposes, and about the effect of sport in culture. I had found what I was looking for: connection, affirmation, information, and validation. This man has spent his entire career within anthropology forming and researching these ideas, and they fit perfectly within the context of sportuality. Because anthropology is defined as the study of humanity, with roots in social sciences, natural sciences, and humanities, I see it as another version of the trinity of mind, body, and spirit.

## Sport's Sacred Spaces

When Kalamazoo College interviewed candidates to serve as a new chaplain, I, as the associate chaplain, had the opportunity to visit individually with each prospect. One applicant had been a hockey player who wrote about sport, and as our conversation developed, it turned to sport venues. He remarked that, to him, an ice rink was a sacred space. How so? He explained that the uniforms were like vestments; the lacing of the skates was a striving for perfection in order to avoid blisters and foot pain; freshly resurfaced ice has the purity of a gold chalice; the player's entrance onto this special surface with whispering skates is a ritual that only those with proper footwear are allowed to perform; and the aroma of the cold, crisp air is like a stone-carved monastery or catacomb. He said that an ice rink is an environment that engages all the senses.

But of course! I mentally went back to the small gym in the basement of our volleyball practice venue at the University of Michigan where we experienced several off-season and summer practice sessions. Large enough for only one volleyball court, it housed our team perfectly, just as a cozy chapel comforts a small prayer group. Entrance always required donning our special volleyball footwear and kneepads. The ritual of warm-up was a prerequisite for our subsequent opportunities to learn and grow together in solidarity (brotherhood or sisterhood, to use clerical terms).

Our coach was like a pastor. There was ritual, responses, growth, connection. And I felt joy because there was no other single activity I anticipated more during those years than going to the gym to connect with my teammates. Then to have found a career—or actually to have had the career find me—in which I am able to enter that sacred space on a regular basis with people I love is for me like being in heaven.

I believe if we remain in sport, any sport, for any period of time, that the venue becomes us, that it becomes a sacred space that brings meaning, purpose, and, yes, joy into this world. It's where we experience connection to community on a regular basis. There is even a schedule to confirm the validity of our commitment to meet in the appointed sanctuary—either our home court or that of the other team.

## My Sanctuary: Tiger Stadium

Tiger Stadium, the former home of the Detroit Tigers, in downtown Detroit—at the intersection of Michigan and Trumbull, is a sanctuary story. My husband, Jim, and I went there on several occasions, the first being my birthday during our first year together in 1981, and the last being on our wedding anniversary in June 2010. It's a field now. The stadium is gone, and walking there was like walking into a haunted house. The ghosts (memories) that live there no longer have a home. The once-manicured lawn and infield has gone to weeds. You can see where home plate used to be, but there's nothing of beauty left there. I cried.

I remember my eighth birthday. My parents were both Tiger fans, and the only thing I wanted for a present was tickets to a Tigers game. I'd seen games on television, but they were in black-and-white, and I wanted to see what it was really like—in person. I got my wish. My dad took me. I remember the grass and the thousands of people and the bigness of it all. But most of all, I remember the grass. It was greener than I thought grass could ever be. My dad looked at me and said, "It's green, isn't it?"

If you've never seen the expanse of natural green turf at a major league ballpark, my dad's rhetorical question might sound inane. But if you understand the sanctuarial spirit of such a scene, you know my dad was speaking a simple truth, and you understand that all I could say, with mouth agape and eyes wide, was, "Yeah."

During that game, I had to get used to not having Ernie Harwell's mellow baritone voice, tinged with a hint of southern drawl, telling me the play-by-play. I had to get used to experiencing the action for myself, to being a part of it rather than separated from it or linked by only a staticky AM radio transmission.

If you've ever stood in a moment of reverence on your special football or soccer field, you know what I mean. If you've ever walked the distance of a horserace track or the oval of a motor speedway, you know. If you've ever been alone on a volleyball court and run your fingers along the net or been alone on a basketball court with a ball lying idle nearby, picked it up, and taken a shot just because you wanted to, you know. If you read this and understand, you know, don't you? The grass is green, the oval is smooth, the net is tactile, the hardwood is shiny—the sanctuary is real. Isn't it?

If you nod or say yes, you know that what you are experiencing is the spirit of the game, the spirit of the stadium, the sanctuary. It's the spirit of sport burning inside you as a human and as a fan.

My husband, Jim, has memories of being at Tiger Stadium in 1962 when the Yankees had Mickey Mantle, Roger Maris, Yogi Berra, and Whitey Ford, but the memory for him lies in seeing his hero, Tiger Rocky Colavito, hit a home run. Jim's dad took him to his first professional game there. He knows. My mom has stories of going to Tiger Stadium with her neighbor as a child growing up in Detroit in the 1930s. She is still a fan. She knows. My dad also grew up in Detroit and worked just blocks from Tiger Stadium for years. The Tigers are in his blood. He knows. My sons, Andrew and Kevan, attended *their* first Tiger games there with their dad. They know. I am now Facebook friends with Tiger Stadium. I know.

My friend Robert Weir, who edited and helped me craft this book, tells of going to Tiger Stadium as a teenager and catching two balls, and almost three, during batting practice. And, as a little leaguer, going with a troupe of boys and dads every year on a Saturday afternoon (courtesy of the Tigers), sitting in the leftfield bleachers, each boy three seats apart, and each grasping the front edge of a wooden painted green seat in each hand, lifting them up and slamming them down—up and down, up and down, up and down, up and down, up and down—in cadence, cheering the Tigers in this rhythmic way and making so much noise the adults couldn't stand it. He knows.

Once the Tigers moved to their new home at nearby Comerica Park, those of us who grew up in the spiritual shadow of Tiger Stadium were inspired by efforts to save it. People formed groups. They protested at the site and to the Detroit City Council. Michigan senior Senator, Carl Levin, convinced the U.S. Congress to give millions of dollars to save it, but the cost of renovation would require millions more. Volumes have been published about the rich history and the near-salvation of Tiger Stadium. Some say the owners didn't want to save it no matter how much money might be put into it. So the grand old lady at the corner of Michigan and Trumbull was pulled down and converted into rubble on September 21, 2009. She had stood there since April 28, 1896—113 years, 104 seasons before giving way to the brand new Comerica Park in 2000.[147]

And while the Tigers' new home is a beautiful place—with green, green grass, too—those of us who treasure the sanctuary of Tiger Stadium are sad to see the old stadium gone. But, you know, there's something about the spirit of a place—if it touches enough people— that allows that place to live on. That's what's happening at the corner of Michigan and Trumbull.

A professionally crafted sign on a fence there reads: "Keep the Corner Alive." In gravestone fashion, it says: "In Memory of Tiger Stadium" and includes the dates that mark the structures lifespan: "April 28, 1896-September 21, 2009." It concludes: "Gone but not forgotten!" In addition, someone has written a rest-in-peace tribute to the Tigers' long-time and most revered broadcaster, Ernie Harwell, who died on May 4, 2010.

Inside that fenced area, people are still finding sanctuary. Grassroots citizens are rebuilding the field into a shrine. A newly formed Tiger Stadium Historical Society and supporters raised the American flag on a 125-foot flagpole at the stadium site, calling it "a fitting tribute to the memory of Historic Tiger Stadium and a symbol of past Opening Day celebrations."[148]

---

TIME-OUT:

Go to www.strandedatthecorner.com and watch the video of Tiger Stadium fans clearing and leveling the field with shovels and rakes, placing bases and chalking base paths, and playing ball there today. The people on the video express the same emotion I feel about that particular sanctuary: tears at the demise of the structure, joy over the public interest, and hope for a future sanctioned memorial there at The Corner.

---

# The Calling of Sanctuary

Carrie Brankiewicz graduated from Kalamazoo College in 2004 with a degree in biology and French and a four-season collegiate career in volleyball. She was to begin student teaching in biology at a local high school that following fall. During the summer, she confided that being in a traditional classroom setting didn't feel right: "Coach, I want to spend the rest of my life *in a gym!*" Say no more; I understood. "Well then *do* it," I said. As with me, and now for Carrie, the gym is her sanctuary.

She became an assistant coach in our program while she worked toward certification in personal training, Pilates, and massage therapy. She opened her own fitness studio in downtown Kalamazoo in 2007 while becoming a popular physical education activity class teacher at the college.

Carrie was destined to be in a gym. Her enthusiasm for sport, for training, and for the pursuit of physical nirvana affected students and people of the community. Some might say that she sacrificed job security and financial comfort to dive into the entrepreneurial unknown, but in the gym, her sacred space, she finds a wholeness—holiness—that brings health and fitness to others.

A true competitor, an inspiration, and a joy-filled person, Carrie shares both my desire in sport as well as enthusiasm for my faith tradition. We understand that one enhances the other, that we experience not a dedication to either sport *or* spirituality but that our lives are joined by both—sportuality.

Annie Bianco-Ellett was drawn to her sanctuary, and then another previously unknown sanctuary, in a different way. Annie's known sanctuary was the saddle, and she is well-known in the equestrian world for her astounding accomplishments: World Champion Cowgirl of the Cowboy Mounted Shooting Association (CMSA) and Overall World Champion of the Single Action Shooting Society (SASS). As the only woman to win an overall world championship and a member of the prestigious Cimarron Firearms Team of World Champions, Annie—who performs under the name Outlaw Annie—is perhaps the most recognized person in the cowboy mounted shooting world, which is a male-dominated sport. She has been featured on ESPN, Outdoor Life Network, TNN, and Fox Sports Television. Articles, including cover features about Annie, have appeared in numerous books and worldwide magazines. She was inducted into the CMSA Hall of Fame in 2007, and her horse, El Costa Prom, is the winningest horse in the sport of mounted shooting.[149]

An article in *Phoenix Woman* magazine credits Annie with: "Not only does she command a male-dominated sport, she expertly balances motherhood and family with numerous successful business ventures," which include training riders, breeding horses, acting as a stunt double in feature films, playing a role on a hit reality cowboy show, designing leather and holsters—the industry-leading Outlaw Annie Collection—and competing on the mounted shooting circuit, the latter of which, according to the article, "entails navigating a series of obstacles and breaking ten balloons with her six-guns, all on horseback. And Annie does that in less than ten seconds."[150]

> TIME-OUT:
>
> Go to: http://www.outlawannie.com/bio.htm and take a glimpse of her remarkable precision shooting. Prepare to be amazed!

Annie's path crossed with mine when I had to call her to tell her that we were cancelling the volleyball camp for fourth and fifth graders scheduled for the summer of 2008 due to low numbers. The handwriting on the registration form was that of a fourth grader, in pink. I called the number and reached Annie in Arizona, hundreds of miles from Kalamazoo College in Michigan. Annie explained that her brother Paul lives in Kalamazoo and that he thought this opportunity would be perfect for his niece Sierra, Annie's daughter, and had forwarded the camp flyer to their address. It was going to be the exact time that the Ellets were going to be in Michigan visiting family. So on that first phone call, Annie explained how Sierra was looking forward to the camp so much that she had filled in the form when it arrived in the mail and had Annie mail it back that day. Not wanting to disappoint a budding volleyball enthusiast, I and my team met with and taught Sierra on her visit to Kalamazoo that year and have done so each summer since. Sierra is currently "getting" volleyball, much to my delight, as a leader on her club team in Arizona. I feel sportually connected to both Annie and Sierra through our original meeting and the regular encounters and communication since.

Like Carrie, Annie chose the sportual life over an indoor job. "I had a BA in marketing and a minor in broadcasting. I started as an executive. I worked in both TV and business in New York City. But it just wasn't me. I preferred to go to Central Park and ride horses. I put my passion for horses and the West and my business sense together and found a niche market," she told *Phoenix Woman*. She added, "I think you have to do something you love that really drives you."[151]

That's the same message that Carrie came to realize about the power of calling to a sanctuary.

Armed Forces Entertainment, the agency within the Department of Defense responsible for providing entertainment to U.S. military personnel overseas, invited Annie to go to Iraq to talk with U.S. soldiers there during the week of Memorial Day 2010. She was part of a team of equestrians on the Wrangler (blue jeans) National Patriot Tour; the purpose, according to *Rundown* magazine, the official journal of CMSA, in July 2010, was "to show our men and women in uniform that we care and appreciate the sacrifices they are making for our country."[152]

During that tour, she encountered a sanctuary that is thousands of years old that moved her to her core. She shared how moved she was to find that the monastery that, for centuries, held the spiritual practice of holy men was now the headquarters for war strategy. While some might consider this an evolving use of a structure, it is hardly serving its original intent.

## Sanctuary Rituals

Likewise, as a coach, my life is joined to alumni, current players, and future players by this phenomenon of sportuality. Each year at Homecoming, alumni join us in a ritual at mid-court where we, along with the current team, join hands in a circle and acknowledge our love for the game and each other. For me, this has become a powerful moment in the course of our season and our program because it demonstrates to ourselves and those in attendance that we are whole: past, present, and future. When an athlete graduates, she has a hard time imagining that she will be a part of our team's future success. Sometimes it is not until years later when she will write, call, or e-mail this revelation that she really is out there with us as well as in our hearts—sportually, on the sacred court.

# A Boyhood Sanctuary

My friend Robert Weir tells of the ritual he and his boyhood neighbors conducted in a field, converted to a baseball diamond, throughout each summer in the small, rural community of Emmett, Michigan, in the 1950s and '60s:

> There was a cadre of six of us who played baseball regularly with another six to ten who showed up periodically. Our field was literally a previously plowed field that the father of two brothers let us use. It was centrally located where each of the six of us could see it from our front yards, and we mowed it every weekend. My father sold farm machinery, so I mowed the outfield on a riding lawn mower while the others took care of the infield and foul territory with their push mowers. We eventually leveled some of the high spots by scalping the soil with our mower blades.

> We built our own backstop with two forty-foot, creosoted telephone poles that a line crew left from a nearby pole replacement project. After the linemen had gone and the poles had been lying in a ditch for two months, we asked our parents' permissions to go and get them. We used one of my dad's tractors and a chain to drag them to the field, cut them in half with a handsaw, dug four holes with shovels and a posthole digger, and planted them in concrete. Then we pitched in our money, went to the local Farm Bureau, bought heavy-gauge fencing, and attached it to the poles ourselves.

> We played ball every Saturday, Sunday, and most weeknights. The community attempted Little League once but it didn't stick. Most of the ball players were us, and we would rather play our own pickup games,

choosing teams among ourselves with the traditional hands on the bat—eagle claw allowed—method.

A Michigan highway ran on an angle nearby and hitting a ball on the road was a home run. The leftfield foul line ran about 450 to 500 feet to the road, but straight-away center was 350 feet. One of the big guys, once we became teenagers, would occasionally poke one that far. Deep rightfield held a huge oak tree that was probably over 100 years old. A ball hit high into that tree was a home run, and one of the stronger left-hand batters would do that fairly often.

That field was my place of joy, a sanctuary where I felt at home, whether batting, fielding, running, or mowing.

Today, the neighborhood is devoid of youth who hold the interest that we did. The field is a field again, completely overgrown with twenty—to thirty-foot oak trees, pine trees, and shorter shrubs. Unkempt weedy grasses come and go with the seasons, reaching thigh-high to an adult. Picker bushes snag pants, socks, and skin with greater efficiency than we snagged grounders. The backstop is still there, but one pole leans to the west at an angle of twenty degrees. I've walked through it several times in recent years. The memories are there, but the sanctuary is not the same.

BOX SCORE: Where are your sacred sport spaces? What makes them holy for you? What rituals feed your sporting soul?

Close your eyes and breathe in the essence of the place. Feel the temperature, smell the smells, recall the sounds, imagine the emotions, love the outcome.

Create here a meditation or ritual that you can use every time you enter into your arena or your gym or go onto your field. Mentally place yourself in this holy place as you put on your footwear, protective gear, or uniform. Create excitement within yourself as you hear the crowd, feel the temperature, smell the environs. Let these sensations bring the emotion of the game to your gut— access the butterflies.

# Sacrifice
## "to make holy"
## (self-giving)

**Sacrifice (sa-kre-fis)**

*noun:*

the offering of something precious to a deity; something offered in sacrifice; a loss or deprivation; in baseball, a bunt or fly ball that allows a base runner to advance while the batter is put out.[153]

*The world will never have lasting peace so long as men reserve for war the finest human qualities. Peace, no less than war, requires idealism and self-sacrifice and a righteous and dynamic faith.*

—John Foster Dulles

*I have worshipped woman as the living embodiment of the spirit of service and sacrifice.*

—Mohandas Gandhi

*If you have a chance to make life better for others and fail to do so, you are wasting your time on Earth. No matter what our station in life, we are here to serve, even if that sometimes means making the greatest sacrifice of all.*

—Roberto Clemente

One time when I was feeling sad about having to miss one of my son's high school golf matches, I said to him, "I'm sorry I can't make it to some of your matches because of my coaching." His reply was precious and unforgettable. "That's okay, Mom. I'm sorry I can't come to more of your games." Sometimes the sacrifice comes from coaching, and sometimes the sacrifice comes from parenting.

But there is always a sacrifice. Something is always being made more whole. Maybe that something is me.

# Redefining the Word

The commonly accepted definition of *sacrifice* is to "give up something:" to sacrifice time to assist another, to sacrifice a weekend or family event for work or an important project, to sacrifice oneself for the common good, to sacrifice one's life to save another's.

In actuality, *sacrifice* comes from Middle English, from Anglo-French, and from Latin *sacrificium*, from *sacr-, sacer* + *facere*, which means quite the opposite: "to make whole, to make holy."[154]

Health and healing is also from this same root. Jesus sacrificed his life; the sacrifice of Abraham; sacrifice of soldiers for country or of parents for their children; of coaches for the team. When we are healthy, when we are healed in mind, body, and spirit, we are whole, we become holy.

That being the case, we can then conclude that the role of a parent is to make our children independent as a step toward interdependence, or mutual growth, with another. By sacrificing, according to the original beneficial definition, I was giving my son freedom to be whole as a golfer. While, in contrast, the current definition would dictate that I expect him to come to my games or that I would expect myself to attend his matches; in actuality, however, either of these choices or situations would actually be inhibiting, debilitating, and would build resentment—not healing.

## Sacrificing to Become Whole

Coaches often say, "If our team stays healthy, we'll be okay." When we consider the original definition of *sacrifice*, this statement takes on a new meaning: "If our team stays whole, we'll attain a greater message of our time together." Likewise, baseball's sacrifice play takes on a new meaning: "When I give up my turn at the bat and a chance for a hit in order advance the runner while making an out, I am giving myself more fully to the good of the team."

We "sacrifice" our bodies for the game. Whether we sacrifice time, energy, money, our health, or an at-bat, we believe we are giving up something, even our very life, for the greater good. When we "take one for the team," we sacrifice for the greater good. As sport infuses its messages into the culture, this idea of sacrifice comes with it. Can we, as agents of our sport and of our culture, inspire others to personal sacrifice? Can we, together, make situations, people, and culture more holy, more whole . . . more healed?

I have always believed that through my profession and my job, I was helping move culture toward the philosophical vision of Title IX, which legislatively institutionalized gender equality within athletics. To that end, my children probably spent a lot more time with their dad, with babysitters, and with relatives than with me, especially during my fall volleyball season.

One of the most difficult things in coaching and parenting is spending significant time with other people's children and less time with your own. I look at the bright side of that and say that I was able to have parenting classes; that is, I would take my lessons from my players' parents—parents whose children "got it," those who understood truth, trust, integrity, communication, and something greater, getting to the One. I am grateful for those parents who shared their children with me; they helped educate me in how to teach my children.

I found that being a parent changed the way I coach forever, and coaching forever changed the way I parent. My mom never played sports and would break out in hives if she ever broke a sweat, but she taught me one of the most valuable lessons of my life with one simple comment. As a young underclass member of my high school volleyball team, most of my playing time was in practice. On one particular game day, Mom mentioned that she would see me at the game. My reply was something like, "I'm not going to play anyway. Why would you want to be there?" To which she replied, "Maybe the coach knows something." Wow. Maybe the coach *knows* something. Maybe the *coach* knows something. While I cannot even remember if I did play that game, I do remember that my mom was there, knowing deep within that I was participating in something much greater than I could know at that point. What I needed to learn was that the coach knows something. I have spent my career trying to understand what the coach knows, and, for *this* coach—me—I know that sport and spirituality are linked beyond words, that games are a universal language of union and connection and sacrifice, and, often, a very public journey into ourselves, our beliefs, and our faith.

I am fortunate to have a position in coaching that has allowed me to have my children with me at times, and, fortunately, they are two boys who would rather be in a gym anyway! As I continue to coach and meet my alumni who played years ago, they are incredulous at the ages of my sons; they seem to think that time stopped when they graduated. They recall those two little gym rats running around, playing ball, pulling the fire alarms. And some remember babysitting for them.

Perhaps as I was busy sacrificing for the team, these players were sacrificing for me—we were helping each other and my sons be more whole and complete. Perhaps according to the current definition of *sacrifice*, which says that sacrifice means to give of oneself, my ideas of coaching are backward. Perhaps I do it for my own growth, to make myself more holy. But—and this is the hard part to understand— perhaps in that act of growing and gaining my wholeness, my world is also made more whole.

# Jackie Robinson's Sacrifice

Jackie Robinson made a sacrifice of self, family, anonymity, and comfort for the greater good. As the first African American baseball player in Major League Baseball, Robinson broke baseball's color line when he debuted with the Brooklyn Dodgers in 1947. Through that courageous benchmark act, he was instrumental in bringing an end to racial segregation in professional baseball, which had relegated African Americans to the Negro leagues since the birth of the sport. The example of his character and unquestionable talent challenged the traditional basis of segregation, which challenged many other aspects of American life and contributed significantly to the Civil Rights Movement in the United States. As Robinson said of legislative and cultural equality for Negros and other minorities, "The right of every American to first-class citizenship is the most important issue of our time."[155]

Robinson's actions and class in all matters of baseball reflect the history of the American story, civil rights, and rules about not speaking negatively regardless of the situation. As Robinson made his debut in National League parks around the country, he was ridiculed with catcalls and slurs. But he took it gracefully and with determination to just play the game and let his bat and glove do the talking. Was this sacrifice? Did Robinson gain or lose by performing his role in baseball and society. Jackie, himself, mused, "The way I figured it, I was even with baseball and baseball with me. The game had done much for me, and I had done much for it."[156]

# The Quiet Sacrifice

George Bernard Shaw said, "The real moment of success is not the moment apparent to the crowd." Perhaps it is in quieter times of solitude or one-on-one conversation when the realization of sacrifice occurs.

I had a player who wasn't the most talented, biggest, fastest, or most experienced. But she had something else greater, a *je ne sais quoi* that allowed her to sacrifice on a daily basis at practice and to sit on the sidelines during contests where she continued to exude joy and positivity. In one particular game, it became apparent to me that the team needed this special quality that she brought, so I put her in the game at a crucial moment.

While I would love to report that we turned the game around and won, that was not the case. The miracle occurred after we returned to campus around midnight when she chose to stay back in the van and talk to me with no crowd around. I thought she might ask why she even went in, but, no, that was not the case. Through her tears, she thanked me for such a wonderful experience not only in the game but with the team. She reaffirmed her love of the team and of our school while I sat there in awe of all the sacrifice that had brought her to be able to process at this level so far beyond ego.

She was glowing, although it was midnight. The loss was a thousand miles away, and joy was sitting right in front of me in a van in a parking lot, far away from any sort of crowd, stats, or public recognition. Maybe the coach does know something; maybe the reserve player knows something even more. Sportuality emerges again.

BOX SCORE: How are you affected by knowing that *sacrifice* really means "to make whole" or "to make holy," rather than to give up something, even your life? Does that definition motivate you to sacrifice more? Do you find greater meaning and purpose in your actions? What, or who, comes to mind when you hear "the greatest sacrifice of all?"

When you apply the modern—giving something up—definition of sacrifice, do you find it more difficult to "give up" something: your body, your ideas, your comfort, your ego? By applying the "make whole" definition, do you see how your sacrifice actually creates a healing situation from which everyone benefits?

When you think of sacrifices you have made for your parents, children, teachers, coaches, neighbors, and friends, can you see how your actions actually contributed to their (or your) wholeness and holiness?

# Two-Minute Warning

Sport is glorious. It embodies "the thrill of victory . . . the agony of defeat . . . the human drama of athletic competition," as pronounced amidst brassy musical fanfare in the introduction to *ABC's Wide World of Sports!*

But before the game is over, let's stop for a moment and assess sport. Sport, especially at the professional level, has its problems—most of them fueled by human greed and out-of-control aspiration for fame and undue wealth. The same can be said for some Olympians who get caught up in the quest for glory more than love of the game.

But then news has a way, in general, of focusing on the tragic—"If it bleeds, it leads," is the precept of sensationalistic reporting and, some say, America's adoration of violence. In reality, news is supposed to be about what's different and unusual; that's what makes it *news*. The stories of a cat being rescued from a tree or someone helping someone across a road are too common to make headlines—thank goodness.

So this book has touched on some negative elements found in sport—drug use, gambling, and scandals—because, unfortunately, those are the news-making elements of sport. But to a much greater extent, the positive aspects, the spirit and essence of sport, competition, athleticism, and the places where games are played have been the focus. We are getting to the JOY!

That's the message I want to convey in this huddle before the game continues. We've done well. There have been some setbacks. But sport is winning—and it always will.

Finish strong!

# Overtime

*Destiny is not a matter of chance, it is a matter of choice.
It is not something to be waited for; it is something to be
achieved.*

—William Jennings Bryan

I go back to the 1960s when all we had were black-and-white TVs and transistor radios to tune in our beloved Detroit Tigers. I loved baseball as a child and, with feminist theory having not yet emerged, I felt called to baseball as strongly as any of my brothers or boyfriends. I played pickle, spud, sandlot, and catch, and I stayed current with all the Tigers, their victories, and their stats. It never occurred to me that, just because I was not of the approved gender to play professionally, I shouldn't be interested in the game and the players. Maybe I knew what lay ahead of me as a mother.

Sometimes we experience "where were you when" moments that etch themselves deeply into our psyches and souls. For me, the memory of where I was when Andrew was drafted has a special meaning. I had spent the day waiting for the call. Nothing. Nope, haven't heard. Glued to the live feed on the Internet. Round six, seven, eight. Increasing frustration. Don't call him. Don't ask. Remain patient. I had an appointment for a massage that afternoon, and, when I arrived, I informed the therapist of the situation and asked if I could leave my cell phone turned on during the session.

The first call was Jim: "Call Andrew. He's feeling pretty bad. Nothing yet." Dreams fading, time passing, be patient. The next call came five minutes later: "Andrew is a Tiger!" The first stage of a dream realized, I trembled with excitement and shed tears of joy on the massage table. What a moment of grace.

Speaking of grace, the end of this book will bookend where it began. At Christmas each year, we have encouraged our boys to write letters to their Aunt Mary presenting the big picture of how their year had gone. This year, Andrew wrote a story, "The Lost Ball," and gifted it to all of us—and now I share the spirit of that story with you. Ultimately, it is about "Amazing Grace" and the idea of being lost and found.

*For my Aunt Mary who inspires me to write something good. And to my parents who taught me to always look up.*

*Once upon the time there was an old farmer who had worked his crops for many years. One day his horse ran away. Upon hearing the news, his neighbors came to visit. "Such bad luck," they said sympathetically.*

*"Maybe," the farmer replied.*

*The next morning, the horse returned, bringing with it three other wild horses. "How wonderful!" the neighbors exclaimed.*

*"Maybe," replied the old man.*

*The following day, his son tried to ride one of the untamed horses, was thrown, and broke his leg. The neighbors again came to offer their sympathy on his misfortune.*

*"Maybe," answered the farmer.*

*The day after, military officials came to the village to draft young men into the army. Seeing that the son's leg was broken, they passed him by. The neighbors congratulated the farmer on how well things had turned out.*

*"Maybe," said the farmer.*

*—Zen Philosophy*

Dear Aunt Mary,

If life is a game of cards, fate shows me a new hand each and every day. Some people view the phenomenon of fate as a series of events that are pure coincidences. The "non-believers" if you will. But ask yourself the question, what is fate? Take a second and really think about it before you read on. Does the definition I just provided come to mind? When I did this experiment, every real world definition that came to mind left fate as nothing more than a natural thing, which simply links past events to the present. But there was something inside me that failed to acknowledge that fate was that simple. There has to be more to the story, more to why I am where I am. Something, you could say, that is almost divine. Now what you choose to set your heavenly eye to has no bearing on my thoughts about why things happen. But think about it. The thought that something else has already mapped out my existence and I am just along for the ride seems silly. If that was the case, I could sit on the couch all day and just wait for things to happen. More than I already do, just to note. This logic seems too simple; *you* make your life and live with the decisions you make and directions you decide to go, right? While I may generalize and say that "some people" don't think fate exists or just simply fail to recognize it, I can say for certain that whoever "they" may be, are wrong, at least in my opinion. I know that one event can change your life and that it happens for a reason. One specific event, so small it should have been overlooked. To me, fate is both good and bad. That's simply the way the world works. I was fortunate enough to see both sides of the spectrum resulting from the same event, and still feel the same gratitude and utter thankfulness about my past. The story I have to tell is one about fate and how one event, one day, one swing of a golf club changed my life. At the time, I felt like my life was over, and I had no idea what I was going to do. Never did I stop and think that what happened was for a reason, and that it would make me happier than I could possibly imagine. It took awhile to grasp this logic and accept that things don't just happen and that's the end. It took the people who loved me most to get me to move on. When something happens that affects your life, whether good or bad, understand it happened for a reason. It had to happen. It is how you move on and make the best of the result that will ultimately determine your feelings about fate.

Andrew then goes on to write Aunt Mary a story about fate, sport, love, and luck in which he loses a ball during his last high school golf competition, loses the tournament and a bid to the state championship by one stroke, and ends up at the University of Michigan playing baseball instead. It was there where he would meet the love of his life and ultimately be drafted into the Detroit Tiger organization. He speaks of the joy in that process in the concluding paragraph of *The Lost Ball*:

I owe the life I have now to that one little ball with the two green dots. The ball that started off with so much promise, and then was lost, and then found again. So as I began, fate is something you can't explain why it happens. But I know for a fact that I was meant to meet Amanda, and I was meant to play for the Tigers. These were not things that I set out to accomplish before I lost that ball. Fate is a real thing, and I don't know what or who makes it happen. Is it God? Is it your own reactions to life's situations? Whatever it is a person may believe, God, no God, hard work, luck, it makes no difference. All that matters is that things happen for a reason, sometimes for reasons unknown, but over time all things are always revealed.

BOX SCORE:

Have you ever received anything from something you thought you lost? Where is your lost ball? What is your season-ending injury story? Did your life begin anew?

Where is your joy? Consider your sportual life and how the spirit of the games has shaped your thoughts, your words, and your experiences.

# Victory
## "to emerge"
## (perseverance)

**Victory (vik-te-ree)**

*noun:*

the overcoming of an enemy or antagonist; achievement of mastery or success in a struggle or endeavor against odds or difficulties.[157]

*No compromise with the main purpose, no peace till victory, no pact with unrepentant wrong.*

—Winston Churchill

*Glory lies in the attempt to reach one's goal and not in reaching it.*

—Mohandas Gandhi

*In baseball, the victorious team is the one with the most players safe at home.*

—Robert M. Weir

"I had no earthly idea when I sat down to create *Sportuality* that we would reach this day." The *this day* has occurred several times: on the day I shared the manuscript with a peer review group, the day we finished the final edits, the day the manuscript was accepted by a publisher, the day it was actually printed, bound, and released to the public. And *this day* is happening now, again, as you read these words. This moment is a moment of victory.

The victory is our greater mutual awareness of the words we have redefined and the concepts we have reexamined throughout the course of this book.

Communication ("to make common"), Spirit ("to breathe"), Competition ("to work with"), Community ("to have charge of together"), Humor ("to be fluid and flexible like water"), Enthusiasm ("to know God within"), Education ("to draw forth"), Religion ("to link back, to connect"), Holy ("to become One"), Sanctuary ("to honor our holy places"), and Sacrifice ("to make holy").

This moment is a moment of victory for both of us.

## Redefining the Word

The words *victory* and *victor* originated in Latin and came into our language through the Middle English. Much like the way these words are used today, victory means "winning," and victor (or victors) references "the one(s) who overcome or defeat an adversary, the winner(s) of any struggle or contest, conqueror(s)." In ancient Rome, Victor (with a capital V) was an epithet applied to the gods Jupiter, Mars, and Hercules.[158]

Because time has not altered the usage of these words, as was the case with the other words we have redefined throughout this book, we need to then redefine *the reader*. Let's look at who is involved in the struggle or contest, who the adversaries might be, who are the protagonist and the antagonist.

Cartoonist Walt Kelly created two posters that depict his famous character Pogo that read: "We have met the enemy and he is us."[159] "The Enemy Within" is the title of a book, magazine articles, and a *Star Trek* episode. Many people have come to realize that "we are our own worst enemies" or "our own worst critics."

To be victorious also means to "win over," as in to persuade or get someone to see our point of view. Sometimes, the hardest person for us to win over or persuade is the one staring back at us from the mirror. Sometimes, it's just plain hard to see our own self worth.

But when we do, we throw off all outer coverings that hide our true inner spirit and we emerge—victorious.

## Personal Victories

Former major league pitcher and Chicago Cubs' broadcaster Steve Stone found his winning—or victory—deep within his thought process. "I used to try not to lose before," he told Henry Hecht of the *New York Post* before starring in the 1980 All-Star game in Los Angeles during his Cy Young award-winning season. "Now, when I go out, I go out to win every time, and I'm certain I am. I try to envision myself literally walking off the mound a winner. I allow no negatives in my thinking. When certain ones start creeping in, I erase them and make it like a blank blackboard waiting to be filled in with things like, 'The team is going to play well, is going to score some runs, I'm going to throw strikes, I'm going to win'."[160]

The ultimate victory is that which comes from deep within, such as the victory spirit shown by the softball players who helped their competitor around the bases after she hit a home run and tore her ACL going around first. This seemingly right and simple act won the 2008 ESPY award for sportsmanship and is now on the "pass it on" series billboards around the country, motivating us to be better people.

I think back to my former player Dawn, who experienced tearing her ACL in a similar manner between first and second and getting the ride of her life through a message into hope, joy, and optimism. Lastly, I think of the ultimate storyteller Jimmy Buffett, who had helped me through my banquet, and his famous line from "Growing Older But Not Up": "I rounded first, never thought of the worst, as I studied the shortstop's position. Crack went my leg, like the shell of an egg. Someone call a decent physician."

Maybe there is something to this *rounding first.* We're participating in the game. We're on the journey, moving forward and heading toward the safety of home—the home that is within ourselves.

We've exhibited a skill and had some success to get to that point— to first base. And now the only way to win the game is to keep moving. It is those moments in any sport—when we round first—that we get a small scent of victory for all.

---

**BOX SCORE:**

Where have your greatest victories been? Have they been within sport, or elsewhere? Did sport have anything to do with those moments? Are you inspired to victory in other areas of your life because of your participation in or awareness of sport?

Can you see the role of sport in cultural evolution and yourself as an active participant?

Do you and can you understand sport as the victor, and, within that, can you access the joy that is available to us free and clear on a daily basis?

Got Joy?

# Endnotes

1. *Dictionary.com*, s.v. "sport," accessed April 20, 2010, http://dictionary.reference.com/browse/sport.

2. *Dictionary.com*, s.v. "spiritual," accessed April 20, 2010, http://dictionary.reference.com/browse/spritual.

3. *Dictionary.com*, s.v. "spirituality," accessed April 20, 2010, http://dictionary.reference.com/browse/spirituality.

4. Christina Baldwin, "Storycatcher: Making Sense of Our Lives through the Power and Practice of Story," *New World Library: Books That Change Lives*, http://www.newworldlibrary.com/ArticleDetails/tabid/230/ArticleID/17/Default.aspx, (accessed April 2009).

5. *Dictionary.com*, s.v. "ode," accessed April 8, 2010, http://dictionary.reference.com/browse/ode.

6. *Dictionary.com*, s.v. "joy," accessed April 8, 2010, http://dictionary.reference.com/browse/joy.

7. Malcolm Gladwell, *Outliers: The Story of Success*, (Little, Brown and Company, 2008).

8. Matthew 7:7-8.

9. Dianna Booher, *The Little Book of Big Questions: Answers to Life's Perplexing Questions*, (J. Countryman, 2001), 67.

10. Leon Bloy, Ibid, 67.

11. Irma Zaleski, *Who Is God? The Soul's Road Home*, (New Seeds Books, 2003), 88.

12. Rabindranath Tagore, (1861-1941) winner of the Nobel Prize in Literature in 1913.

13. Alexander Wolff, "The Audacity of Hoops: How basketball helped shape Obama," SI.com, http://sportsillustrated.cnn.com/2009/writers/alexander_wolff/01/13/obama/index.html (accessed February 2009).

14. Mark Nepo, "About Joy," from Reduced to Joy, Mark Nepo, p. 8, in manuscript, by permission of the author.

15. Phil Jackson, *Sacred Hoops*, (New York, NY: Hyperion, 1995), xii.

16. Ibid, xiii.

17. *Dictionary.com*, s.v. "communication," accessed April 10, 2010, http://dictionary.reference.com/browse/communication.

18. Bert Jacobs and John Jacobs, *Life Is Good: Simple Words from Jake and Rocket,* (Meredith Books, 2007), no pagination.

19. Steve Bhaerman and Bruce Lipton, *Spontaneous Evolution*, (Hay House, 2009), 4.

20. Marianne Williamson, *Meditations for a Miraculous Life,* (Hay House, Audio CD 2007), Morning Meditation.

21. Madisyn Taylor, Words Have Weight, *DailyOM—Inspirational Thoughts for a Happy, Healthy and Fulfilling Day,* http://www.dailyom.com/articles/2010/22176.html (accessed February 16, 2010). Register for free at www.dailyom.com.

22. Ibid.

23. Ibid.

24. George Carlin, "Baseball versus Football," YouTube, http://www.youtube.com/watch?v=om_yq4L3M_I (accessed January 2010).

25. Hermann Goering. Gledhill Enterprises, 2011, http://www.great-quotes.com/quote/5732 (accessed December 7, 2011).

26. Steve Bhaerman and Bruce Lipton, *Spontaneous Evolution,* (Hay House, 2009), 345.

27. *Dictionary.com*, s.v. "spirit," accessed April 18, 2010, http://dictionary.reference.com/browse/spirit.

28. Genesis 2:7.

29. "ESPY Award Winners," *ESPN*, http://sports.espn.go.com/espn/news/story?id=3493330 (accessed May, 2009).

30. "Central Washington offers the ultimate act of sportsmanship," *ESPN College Sports*, http://sports.espn.go.com/ncaa/columns/story?id=3372631 (accessed May, 2009).

31. "Softball player carried around bases by opponents," *YouTube* http://www.youtube.com/watch?v=xVlKtI7yd_s (accessed May, 2009).

32. "CWU Softball Players Mallory Holtman and Liz Wallace Win ESPY for Best Moment," *seattle pi*, http://blog.seattlepi.com/spi/2008/07/21/cwu-softball-players-mallory-holtman-and-liz-wallace-win-espy-for-best-moment/ (accessed May, 2009).

33. "Shamanism: Working with Animal Spirits," *Animal Spirits*, http://www.animalspirits.com/index5.html (accessed May 2009).

34. "Spirit Guide Healers," *Connecting With Your Spirit Guides*, http://www.rajunasrefuge.com/guidehealers.html (accessed May, 2009).

35. Terry Pettit, "After the Loss," *Talent and the Secret Life of Teams*, (Terry Pettit, 2008), 55, used with permission.

36. Alexander Wolff, "The Audacity of Hoops: How basketball helped shape Obama," http://sportsillustrated.cnn.com/2009/writers/alexander_wolff/01/13/obama/index.html (accessed February, 2009).

37. Barack Obama, *Dreams from My Father*, (Three Rivers Press, 2004), 79.

38. Alexander Wolff, "The Audacity of Hoops: How basketball helped shape Obama," http://sportsillustrated.cnn.com/2009/writers/alexander_wolff/01/13/obama/index.html (accessed February 2009).

39. Ibid.

40. Ibid.

41. Ibid.

42. National Collegiate Athletic Association, news release, September 1, 2009, www.sports.espn.go.com (accessed August 15, 2009—Link no longer functional).

43. Ibid.

44. Barack Obama, "on the essence of the Olympic spirit," Presentation to the International Olympic Committee, October 2, 2009. Olympic Spirit, Olympic Spirit. http://www.olympicspirit.org/index2.php (accessed April 2010).

45. International Olympic Committee, Olympic Spirit, http://olympicspirit.org/ (accessed April 2010 ).

46. "Jamaica original bobsled," YouTube, http://www.youtube.com/watch?v=qIHjLTDTEqE&watch response (May 2010).

47. Galatians 5:22—23.

48. WayneTeasdale, *The Mystic Heart: Discovering a Universal Spirituality in the World's Religions*, (Novato, CA, New World Library, 1999), 11. Reprinted with permission of New World Library, Novato, CA. www.newworldlibrary.com.

49. Patsy Neal, *Sport and Identity*, (Philadelphia, PA, Dorrance, 1972).

50. Luke 11:9 and Matthew 7:7.

51. *Dictionary.com*, s.v. "competition," accessed April 19, 2010, http://dictionary.reference.com/browse/competition.

52. *Dictionary.com*, s.v. "compete," accessed April 19, 2010, http://dictionary.reference.com/browse/compete.

53. HBO Documentary, http://www.hbo.com/sports/battle-for-tobacco-road-duke-vs-carolina/index.html (accessed April 2010).

54. Steve Bhaerman and Bruce Lipton, *Spontaneous Evolution,* (Carlsbad, CA, Hay House, 2009), 202.

55. Ibid, 126.

56. Ibid, 44.

57. Michael Dwinell, *God-Birthing: Toward Sacredness, Personal Meaning, and Spiritual Nourishment,* (St. Louis, MO, Liguori Publications, 1994). http://www.spiritualityandpractice.com/books/excerpts.php?id=13711.

58. Eckhart Tolle, *The Power of Now,* (Novato, CA, New World Library, 1999), 30.

59. Steve Bhaerman and Bruce Lipton, *Spontaneous Evolution,* (Carlsbad, CA, Hay House, 2009), 173.

60. Marianne Williamson, *Illuminata,* (New York, NY, Riverhead Books, 1994), 189.

61. Ibid, 189.

62. Phil Jackson, *Sacred Hoops,* (New York, NY: Hyperion, 1995), 175.

63. Ken Burns, *Baseball,* Public Broadcasting Service, http://www.pbs.org/kenburns/baseball/ documentary (accessed March 2010).

64. "Interview with Rachel Robinson," Scholastic, February 11, 1991, http://www2.scholastic.com/browse/article.jsp?id=4808 (accessed September 2010).

65. Terry Pettit, "After the Loss," *Talent and the Secret Life of Teams,* (Terry Pettit, 2008), 55. Used with permission.

66. *Dictionary.com,* s.v. "community," accessed April 22, 2010, http://dictionary.reference.com/browse/community.

67. Wayne Teasdale, *The Mystic Heart: Discovering a Universal Spirituality in the World's Religions,* (Novato, CA, New World Library, 1999), 115. Reprinted with permission of New World Library, Novato, CA. www.newworldlibrary.com.

68. Donella Meadows, "The Laws of the Earth and the Laws of Economics," Sustainability Institute, The Donella Meadows Archive, http://www.sustainer.org/dhm_archive/index.php?display_article=vn674economics%26earthed (accessed February 12, 2011).

69. Jaime Diaz, "Playing With Heart: Pebble Beach's top teacher wants to chokeproof your game," Golf Digest, May 2007 http://www.golfdigest.com/magazine/2007-05/diaz_heart (accessed June 2009).

70. David Breslow, "The Heart of the Matter," Golf Channel, June 26, 2008, http://www.thegolfchannel.com/golf-fitness/the-heart-of-the-matter-26406/ (accessed June 2009).

71. Lisa Kocian, "Fanning the Flames: Red Sox devotees share their quirks as camera rolls for a film project," boston.com, August 10, 2008, http://www.boston.com/news/local/articles/2008/08/10/fanning_the_flames/ (accessed December 2009).

72. Yogi Berra, "Yogi Berra Quotes," Baseball Almanac, http://www.baseball-almanac.com/quotes/quoberra.shtml (accessed March 12, 2010).

73. Phil Jackson, *Sacred Hoops*, (New York, NY: Hyperion, 1995), 173.

74. John Wooden, *Wooden: A Lifetime of Observations and Reflections On and Off the Court*, (New York, NY, McGraw-Hill Companies, 1997), 120.

75. Ibid, 121.

76. Joseph Chilton Pearce, *The Death of Religion and the Rebirth of the Spirit: A Return to the Intelligence of the Heart*, (Rochester, VT, Park Street Press, 2007), with permission, www.InnerTraditions.com.

77. Joe Falls, *Detroit Free Press*, October 11, 1968.

78. Dan Ewald, *John Fetzer: On A Handshake*, (Champaign, IL: Sagamore Publishing, 1977), 151.

79. Nelson Mandela, http://www.aipsmedia.com/index. php?page=news&cod=523&tp=n (accessed June, 2010).

80. Theodore Roosevelt, "The Man in the Arena," Excerpt from the speech "Citizenship In A Republic", delivered at the Sorbonne, in Paris, France on April 23, 1910.

81. William Ernest Henley, "Invictus," 1875.

82. Joseph Blatter, FIFA President, open letter. http://www.fifa.com/worldcup/archive/southafrica2010/news/newsid=1273207/index.html (accessed June, 2010).

83. Conrad Kottak, *Cultural Anthropology,* (New York, NY, McGraw-Hill, 2008).

84. *Dictionary.com,* s.v. "enthusiasm," accessed May 3, 2010, http://dictionary.reference.com/browse/enthusiasm.

85. Eckhart Tolle, *Oneness With All Life,* (New York, NY, Penguin Group, 2008) 105.

86. Matthew 25:14-30; Luke 19:12-28.

87. "Eddie Gaedel," Baseball Library.com, http://www.baseballlibrary.com/ballplayers/player.php?name=eddie_gaedel_1925 (accessed September 22, 2010).

88. Matthew 18:1-4.

89. Matthew 6:33.

90. "Mark Fidrych," *Wikipedia,* http://en.wikipedia.org/wiki/Mark_Fidrych (accessed September 22, 2010).

91. *Dictionary.com,* s.v. "humor," accessed April 22, 2010, http://dictionary.reference.com/browse/humor.

92. *Merriam-Webster,* s.v. "humor," accessed April 22, 2010, http://www.merriam-webster.com/dictionary/humor.

93. WayneTeasdale, *The Mystic Heart: Discovering a Universal Spirituality in the World's Religions,* (Novato, CA, New World Library, 1999), 143-144. Reprinted with permission of New World Library, Novato, CA. www.newworldlibrary.com.

94. Daniel Herwitz, Michigan Today, http://michigantoday.umich.edu/2009/03/story.php?id=7390 (accessed March 4, 2009).

95. Laughter and Health—Some Background Reading, smile of the decade.co.uk, http://www.smileofthedecade.co.uk/health1.html (accessed April 2010).

96. Steve Bhaerman, interview April 2010.

97. "Lil' Red," *Wikipedia*, http://en.wikipedia.org/wiki/Lil'_Red (accessed September 23, 2010).

98. "Stanford Cardinal". *Wikipedia,* http://en.wikipedia.org/wiki/Stanford_Cardinal (accessed September 23, 2010). Photo 2009-10 version credited to Marc Abrams/Stanford Athletics.

99. "Biography," The Famous SD Chicken, http://www.famouschicken.com/biography.html (accessed September 23, 2010).

100. *Dictionary.com,* s.v. "education," accessed May 10, 2010, http://dictionary.reference.com/browse/education.

101. Parker Palmer, *To Know as We Are Known: Education as a Spiritual Journey,* (San Francisco, CA, Harper & Row, 1983).

102. Michelle Cassou and Stewart Cubley, *Life, Paint, and Passion,* (New York, NY, Tarcher/Putnam,1995), 40.

103. "The Painful Lives of Football Players: Players Must Contend with Countless Surgeries, Chronic Pain and Debilitating Injuries," ABC Good Morning America, January 21, 2006, http://abcnews.go.com/GMA/ESPNSports/story?id=1528986 (accessed September 23, 2010).

104. Jane Leavy, *The Last Boy: Mickey Mantle and the End of America's Childhood,* (New York, NY, Harper/Harper Collins, 2010), 21.

105. "Core Values," NCAA, http://www.ncaa.org/wps/wcm/connect/public/NCAA/About+the+NCAA/Who+We+Are/Core+Values+landing+page Last updated June 29,2010, (accessed May 10, 2010).

106. Joseph McCafferty, "The money bowl: the real competition in big-time college sports is over who can spend the most," *All Business*, August 1, 2006, which references *CFO*, The Magazine for Senior Financial Executives. http://www.allbusiness.com/education-training/extra-curricular-activities/12887872-1.html (accessed September 25, 2010).

107. Ibid.

108. "Facilities: Darrell K Royal—Texas Memorial Stadium," *Texas Longhorns*, http://www.texassports.com/facilities/royal-memorial-stadium.html, (accessed September 25, 2010).

109. "Darrell K Royal—Texas Memorial Stadium," *Wikipedia*, http://en.wikipedia.org/wiki/Darrell_K_Royal_%E2%80%93_Texas_Memorial_Stadium, (accessed September 25, 2010).

110. Joseph McCafferty, "The money bowl: the real competition in big-time college sports is over who can spend the most," *All Business*, August 1, 2006, which references *CFO*, The Magazine for Senior Financial Executives. http://www.allbusiness.com/education-training/extra-curricular-activities/12887872-1.html (accessed September 25, 2010).

111. "Estimated Probability of Competing in Athletics Beyond the High School Interscholastic Level," *National Collegiate Athletic Association*, http://www.ncaa.org/wps/wcm/connect/public/NCAA/Issues/Recruiting/Probability+of+Going+Pro (accessed September 25, 2010).

112. "The Spirit of Curling," *Event Program* http://www.curlingonline.info/?p=6 (accessed May 10, 2010).

113. Jim Moore, *Tales from the Small Time,* (Santa Ana, CA, Seven Locks Press, 2000).

114. NCAA Division III Philosophy Statement, NCAA, www.ncaa.org (accessed May 10, 2010).

115. Ibid.

116. *Dictionary.com*, s.v. "religion," accessed May 10, 2010, http://dictionary.reference.com/browse/religion.

117. David Edwards, *Burning All Illusions: A Guide to Personal and Political Freedom*, (Boston, MA: South End Press, 1996), 62.

118. Wayne Teasdale, *The Mystic Heart: Discovering a Universal Spirituality in the World's Religions*, (Novato, CA, New World Library, 1999), 10-11. Reprinted with permission of New World Library, Novato, CA. www.newworldlibrary.com.

119. 1 Thessalonians 5:17.

120. WayneTeasdale, *The Mystic Heart: Discovering a Universal Spirituality in the World's Religions*, (Novato, CA, New World Library, 1999), 11. Reprinted with permission of New World Library, Novato, CA. www.newworldlibrary.com.

121. Acts 17:28.

122. WayneTeasdale, *The Mystic Heart: Discovering a Universal Spirituality in the World's Religions*, (Novato, CA, New World Library, 1999), 11. Reprinted with permission of New World Library, Novato, CA. www.newworldlibrary.com.

123. Joseph Chilton Pearce, *The Death of Religion and the Rebirth of Spirit*, (Rochester, VT, Park Street Press, 2007), 2, with permission, www.InnerTraditions.com.

124. Ibid, 2

125. Ibid, 162.

126. Joseph L. Price, *From Season to Season: Sports as an American Religion*, (Macon, GA, Mercer University Press, 2001), 223.

127. Joseph Chilton Pearce, *The Death of Religion and The Rebirth of Spirit*, (Rochester, VT, Park Street Press, 2007), 25, www.InnerTraditions.com.

128. "List of sports team names and mascots derived from indigenous people," *Wikipedia*, http://en.wikipedia.org/wiki/List_of_sports_team_names_and_mascots_derived_from_indigenous_peoples, (accessed September 25, 2010).

129. "Hindu deities," *Wikipedia*, http://en.wikipedia.org/wiki/Hindu_deities, (accessed September 25, 2010).

130. "Trimurti," *Wikipedia*, http://en.wikipedia.org/wiki/Trimurti, (accessed September 25, 2010).

131. Rachmiel Frydland, "The Trinity Is Jewish," *Menorah Ministries*, http://www.menorah.org/trinity1.html, reprinted on this web site by permission of The Messianic Literature Outreach, Cincinnati, Ohio (accessed September 25, 2010).

132. Craig A. Forney, *The Holy Trinity of American Sports: Civil Religion in Football, Baseball and Basketball*, (Macon, GA, Mercer University Press, 2010), 189.

133. Matthew Fox, *Meditations with Meister Eckhart*, (Santa Fe, NM: Bear and Co., 1983), 129.

134. Franklin Pierce Adams, "Baseball's Sad Lexicon," *Wikipedia*, http://en.wikipedia.org/wiki/Baseball's Sad Lexicon, (accessed September 25, 2010).

135. Robert N. Bellah, "Civil Religion in America" (*This chapter was written for a* Dædalus *conference on American Religion in May 1966).*

136. Neale Donald Walsch, *Conversations with God, Book 1*, (New York, NY, G.B. Putnam's Sons, 1995), 195.

137. *Dictionary.com*, s.v. "holy," accessed June 5, 2010, http://dictionary.reference.com/browse/holy.

138. Lou Gehrig, "Farewell Speech," *The Official Web Site: Lou Gehrig*, http://www.lougehrig.com/about/speech.htm, (accessed September 26, 2010).

139. Ibid.

140. John Underwood, (lecture at Kalamazoo College, Kalamazoo, MI, October 24, 2010).

141. "Drugs & Sport: 10 Drug Scandals," *CBC Sports Online*, January 19, 2003, http://www.cbc.ca/sports/indepth/drugs/stories/top10.html#1 (accessed September 26, 2010).

142. "Marion Jones," *Wikipedia*, http://en.wikipedia.org/wiki/Marion Jones (accessed September 26, 2010).

143. "Roger Clemens Indicted for Lying to Congress," *CBSSports.com*, August 19, 2010, http://www.cbsnews.com/stories/2010/08/19/sportsline/main6787425.shtml (accessed September 26, 2010).

144. Robert Longley, "Did Congress Have Authority for Baseball Steroid Hearings?" *About.com US Government Info*, http://usgovinfo.about.com/od/uscongress/a/steroids.htm (accessed September 26, 2010).

145. *Dictionary.com*, s.v. "sanctuary," accessed June 6, 2010, http://dictionary.reference.com/browse/sanctuary.

146. Conrad Kottak, *Cultural Anthropology*, (New York, NY, McGraw-Hill, 2008).

147. "Tiger Stadium (Detroit)," Wikipedia, http://en.wikipedia.org/wiki/Tiger_Stadium_(Detroit) (accessed September 23, 2010).

148. "Corner Chatter, Michigan and Trumbull," Preserve Tiger Stadium, http://www.strandedatthecorner.com/ (accessed September 23, 2010).

149. "Annie Bianco-Ellett: World & National Champion," *Outlaw Annie: Annie Bianco-Ellett*, http://www.outlawannie.com/bio.htm (accessed September 26, 2010).

150. Brettan Bablove, "Annie Get Your Gun: Outlaw Annie Bianco-Ellett," *Phoenix Woman* magazine, http://www.phoenixwoman.com/articles/detail/13 (accessed September 26, 2010).

151. Ibid.

152. CMSA Rundown, *CMSA Rundown* magazine, June/July 2010, page 39 (blurb at bottom of page), http://issuu.com/rundown/docs/rdnjunejuly10 (accessed September 26, 2010).

153. *Dictionary.com,* s.v. "sacrifice," accessed June 6, 2010, http://dictionary.reference.com/browse/sacrifice.

154. *Merriam-Webster,* s.v. "sacrifice," accessed June 6, 2010, http://www.merriam-webster.com/dictionary/sacrifice.

155. Jackie Robinson, "Jackie Robinson Quotes: Quotes From & About Jackie Robinson," Baseball Almanac, http://www.baseball-almanac.com/quotes/quojckr.shtml.

156. Ibid.

157. *Dictionary.com,* s.v. "victory," accessed June 6, 2010, http://dictionary.reference.com/browse/victory.

158. Ibid.

159. Walt Kelly first used the quote "We Have Met The Enemy and He Is Us" on a poster for Earth Day in 1970.

160. Steve Stone, *Jews in Sports,* http://www.jewsinsports.org/Publication.asp?titleID=1&current_page=267 (accessed December 2010).

# About the Author

Jeanne Hess was born on the cusp of Title IX, grew up in suburban Detroit as a tomboy in the 1960s, and came of age as a varsity athlete at the University of Michigan in the 1970s. The allure of sports and spirituality was nurtured throughout her twenty-eight-year career as a volleyball coach, professor of physical education, and college chaplain at Kalamazoo College, and by virtue of being the wife of a coach and the mother of two professional athletes.

Raised as a dualistic Catholic-Episcopalian, Jeanne has embraced the universal nature of Catholicism, defining all people as God's children united in spirit. She lives in Kalamazoo, Michigan, with her husband, whom she met in a gym. Their lives have been defined, shaped and enhanced by several different gyms and athletic arenas.

CPSIA information can be obtained
at www.ICGtesting.com
Printed in the USA
LVOW13s0109270717
542811LV00011B/96/P